ALEX
THE LIFE OF A CHILD

FRANK DEFORD

Rutledge Hill Press
Nashville, Tennessee

Copyright © 1983, 1997 by Frank Deford

First published in 1983 by the Viking Press
40 West 23rd Street, New York, N.Y. 10010

Published in Nashville, Tennessee, by Rutledge Hill Press, 211 Seventh Avenue North, Nashville, Tennessee 37219.

Distributed in Canada by H. B. Fenn & Company, Ltd., 34 Nixon Road, Bolton, Ontario L7E 1W2.

Distributed in Australia by The Five Mile Press Pty. Ltd., 22 Summit Road, Noble Park, Victoria 3174.

Distributed in New Zealand by Tandem Press, 2 Rugby Road, Birkenhead, Auckland 10.

Distributed in the United Kingdom by Verulam Publishing, Ltd., 152a Park Street Lane, Park Street, St. Albans, Hertfordshire AL2 2AU.

Portions of this book appeared originally in *People* magazine.

Library of Congress Cataloging-in-Publication Data

Deford, Frank.
  Alex : the life of a child / Frank Deford
      p.   cm
  Originally published : New York : Viking Press, 1983
  ISBN 1-55853-552-7 (pbk.)
    1. Deford, Alexandra, 1971–1980—Health. 2. Cystic fibrosis in children—Patients—United States—Biography. 3. Terminally ill children—United States—Biography. 4. Deford, Alexandra, 1971–1980. I. Title.
  RJ456.C9D43 1997
  362.1'989237—dc21
  [B]   97-26497
                                                                           CIP

Grateful acknowledgment is made to Cydney Slotoroff for permission to reprint the song "Child of the Star," by Cydney Slotoroff. Copyright © 1981 by Cydney Slotoroff.

Printed in the United States of America
Set in Caslon 540

THIS BOOK IS FOR
Tom Dolan and for all the doctors and nurses
who work against cystic fibrosis and

THIS BOOK IS FOR
Doris Tulcin and for all the volunteers
and professionals who work for the
Cystic Fibrosis Foundation.

FOREWORD

This book was first published in 1983, and although the qualities it celebrates—of courage and love and nobility—remain forever to be honored, unchanged, I should note what *is* different now.

There have been many advances in the fight against cystic fibrosis. It remains yet unconquered, still the largest fatal genetic disease in the world. But people who have CF are also born to great hope now. Their life expectancy has doubled, almost tripled, to the age of thirty or so. New medications and more sophisticated treatments allow people with CF to enjoy much fuller lives.

Moreover, we grow closer every day to the cure. In 1989 the CF gene was located, and in the last few years more than one hundred CF patients have participated in gene transplant therapy. Our doctors truly believe that, soon, we can overcome the defective genes. The progress goes far beyond anything I could have imagined in Alex's lifetime—and I want you to keep that in mind about the here and now of cystic fibrosis, as you read this book about a little girl and cystic fibrosis then. We are so near to curing Alex's disease.

—F.D., May 1997

ALEX

DEAR SCARLET,

NOW, WHEN YOU'RE OLD ENOUGH
TO READ THIS, YOU WILL KNOW
ALL ABOUT ALEX. . . .

Alex barely lived eight years. That's not long at all. Why, looking back, it seems as if it took her much longer than that just to die. The dying seemed to take forever. But still, even for all that, for all the time I had to prepare myself, when the end finally came, I wouldn't let it. At the last, I denied that Alex could die. We knew she was going to die, knew she had to, knew there was no hope, even knew it was best. But still, I started telling myself that it was a couple of weeks away.

It's different, a child dying. It isn't just that children are supposed to keep on living. Imagine being eight years old and dead. It isn't just what everybody always says either—that a child dying is unnatural. It's much more than that. Old people die with achievements, memories. Children die with opportunities, dreams. They carry the hopes of all of us when they go off. Probably a child's death is more intolerable for us than for the child. Keep it two weeks away and you have some chance.

Carol and I were actually sitting downstairs, talking about it before going to bed, being straightforward and adult, at precisely that moment when Alex began to die in earnest. "Two weeks," I said. "I feel now she's got about two weeks to go."

1

"Yes, that's just about what I think," Carol said. "Probably sometime in February."

"Yeah, I want to spend more time with Chris, getting him ready for it. I think I'll have a long talk with him on Sunday."

And that was the instant when Alex called out. She had been asleep, but she awoke in pain, unable to breathe. "Help me! Help me!" she cried.

Carol sprang to her feet and dashed up the stairs. I didn't move. I knew what Alex needed and that Carol could provide that, as best she could. *Help me! Help me!*—It was a part of our lives by then. But this time was different as well. I knew that straightaway, as sure as Carol felt it, too. It would not be two weeks after all.

It was not even a day. Alex died in her bed the next afternoon, in my arms, holding her mother's hands.

Later, a doctor came and signed the death certificate, which is filed somewhere, and then the people from the funeral parlor. Carol asked them and our friends to wait in another part of the house, and then I picked up Alex from her bed and carried her out of her room and down the stairs for the last time. Carol and Chris walked with me, with Alex. We left together as a family of four.

That night, by myself, I retraced my steps out the front door. It was incredibly bright out. That was not just my imagination. There was not a cloud to block out a single star; the whole sky positively sparkled. I heard later that it had something to do with the moon and a unique atmospheric condition. Possibly; believe what you will. I only saw that it was extraordinary and was sure that it must have something to do with Alex. And so I walked about, staring up at those starry heavens, where she was spending her first night.

And, as I walked, I poured out a bottle of root beer on the lawn all around the house. I don't even remember Alex caring for root beer one way or the other, but, for some reason, she had asked me, that morning, to go out and get her some. How odd that felt, to go to the store. There were all these other people in the store, going on about their lives, buying things, standing in line, living a Saturday. Alex died on a Saturday. It was so strange, what went on in my mind. I kept thinking there must be something wrong with everybody else in the store, because they weren't buying root beer for a child of theirs, dying back at the house, a few blocks away.

So that's why I had the root beer bottle that night, walking around the house, pouring it out. Alex had only managed a few sips before she died, and I'd bought her a whole quart bottle. Or a liter. Quart or liter. I don't remember whether there were liters yet, in January 1980. But, anyway, there was a lot left, and I couldn't just put it back in the refrigerator, next to the milk and the orange juice. So, it was in the manner of some consecration that I walked about, spreading what was left of the root beer upon the earth where Alex had played.

It was bitter cold and still, the way most winter's nights with clear skies are, and now, finished emptying the bottle, looking up one more time, I suddenly remembered one of my father's favorite quotations, from Shakespeare. He had recited it to me when I was a boy. It was Juliet, talking of her love:

> When he shall die,
> Take him and cut him out in little stars,
> And he will make the face of heav'n so fine
> That all the world will be in love with Night
> And pay no worship to the garish Sun.

Much as I loved to hear my father say that, I could never really visualize the imagery until that night, when I could see Alex up there, cut out in all those stars. So that is the way the day ended when my child died. I said good night to the stars, put the root beer empty in the trash, and went back into the house where the three of us lived.

CHAPTER 1

Even now, so long after she died, even now it's still difficult to go through all the little objects of her life that she left behind. There is not that much that a child leaves, and Alex lived such a short time: small parts of 1971 and 1980, and all of 1972 through 1979, inclusive. She was born, diagnosed, lived all she could, and died before there was time for her to be laden with all the formal artifacts—letters and numbers and citations and all that grown-up bric-a-brac that comes with adult convention and ceremony. But there is not that much for a child. Why, some stranger coming across Alex's stuff would think she must have spent most of her life drawing.

What possesses us to hold onto these cream-colored papers our children scrawl on? I go through sheet after sheet that she attacked with crayons when she was only in nursery school. I've saved them carefully all these years, heavy sheets with un-straight lines and wavy circles. "That's absolutely beautiful, Alex . . . What is it?"

Pause. Young children never have the foggiest notion what they might have drawn. They have drawn un-straight lines and wavy circles. But they humor us. "That's a car." Or, "That's Captain Kangaroo talking on the telephone in his pajamas." And then we rave at their imagination.

Reviewing her work, I can see that Alex did begin to develop some specialties in the art line as she got older: houses (always with smoke curling out of chimneys), bunny rabbits and dogs (you could tell them apart because bunny rabbits were the ones in spring), flowers and trees, both more resembling lollipops, and rainbows. Usually across the top was a ribbon of blue, the sky.

This is, all in all, a very happy collection of items she chose to celebrate, but I am reluctant, even now, to draw any conclusions. When our son, Chris, was in nursery school, we received a very solemn phone call from the teacher asking if we could please come and see her. It was extremely important. Worse, when Carol and I arrived, panicky parents, there was a child psychologist who had been called in, too. He was obviously deeply troubled, and he and the teacher both tiptoed around, asking a lot of careful questions about our home life. It was soon apparent to me, too, that the psychologist was annoyed that we wouldn't admit to any traumas, beatings, or orgies at our house. Finally, he sprung the trap on us. He brought out a drawing Chris had done on the cream-colored paper. It was of a huge, clawed, fanged monster, spitting bullets and fire alike. Terrific picture; best he had ever done. Also, the monster was *stepping on a house*. "Whose house," asked the psychologist. "My house," said Chris. The implications were clear. What did I think? the psychologist asked me.

I said I thought that a monster movie Chris had seen the other evening on television had made a considerable impression on him.

I still have that drawing, too. And all of those that Alex did. Even if they don't mean anything, there isn't much you can save that your child did, even when it's important to you, even when you know she'll die and won't ever obtain all the official clutter that grown-ups do. Of course, there are home movies and a lot of snapshots. These form a pretty complete catalog of Alex's life, too; except because Carol and

I are not real camera addicts, the pictures always come in clusters, a roll now, the child all in the same outfit, and then another six months later, all in another same outfit, probably at a birthday party. And, naturally, nobody ever had any flashbulbs at the right moment. The guilt is overwhelming when you have a child who dies. Even now I say to myself, at least, at least you could have had the flashbulbs.

I have a few recordings of Alex's voice, too, starting when she was almost three, in the fall of 1974, and periodically after. I would sit Chris and Alex down and ask them a few simple questions, and they would respond the best they could, between giggles. What do you like to do best, Alex? "Play house." What do you like to wear? "Long dresses." Mostly they were more interested in hearing themselves played back than in anything they might say. In fact, best of all for them was when the formal interview was finished and I would permit them to make optional noises into the microphone. Also, one whole interview I later erased by mistake. And I always forgot the damn flashbulbs. And then, all of a sudden, she's just gone; there's no more.

The last thing I have of Alex on tape is a recording she made with me one soft, shining day the summer before she died. She loved the silly messages I would make up for my telephone answering machine; I would put on an accent or work up a little bit—instead of just saying please leave your name and number. Alex pleaded with me to include her in the act the next time I made up a message, and so one day, when she was depressed because she had just found out that she had to go back into the hospital, I created a new routine with a good part for her, and we practiced it.

When someone called up and the phone machine went on, the caller heard the shower running. In fact, it really was the shower running, although I'm not sure it sounded like that. Anyway, then Alex came on the microphone, crying out, "Oh, it's the telephone, Dad."

And then I said, "Hey, I'm sorry, all the Defords are in the shower here, but if you'll just leave your name and your number and any message when you hear the beep, after I get out and get dried off and put some baby powder on, I'll call you right back, okay?"

And then the caller heard the shower running again, until just before the beep when Alex yelled, "Pass the soap, Mom!"

She adored doing that with me, and when she had to return to the hospital, we would call back to the house so she could hear herself on the phone machine. "Pass the soap, Mom!"

Alex had a great sense of humor, she loved to act, and I still enjoy going back and listening to that message (I saved it on tape), because, silly as it is, it has charm and life, and those are the memories I want of her.

And I remember too what fun Alex and I had doing it. In fact, when I finished making the tape we were having so much fun that she asked me what I was going to do next, and when I said I didn't have anything special planned, she said we ought to do something else together, and I said sure, fine, what, and she thought awhile, and finally she just said, "Laugh."

And I agreed that was a fine idea. Alex was always a great laugher. After she died, when the children in her class wrote remembrances of her, an unusual number wrote about times she had laughed. Their recollections were about evenly divided between her courage and her laughter, as a matter of fact. She laughed so well it left an impression. For example, Jake Weinstock wrote: "One time in school last year, Stephen Baker made Alex laugh so hard that she fell in my arms and then she laughed even harder. Then we all laughed."

And so then Alex and I laughed. Unfortunately, at that point, late in her life, it was difficult for her to laugh without coughing and starting to choke. So she made sure she

8

laughed gently, and I laughed extra hard, for both of us. Then she came over, sat in my lap, and this is what she said: "Oh, Daddy, wouldn't this have been great?"

That is what she said, exactly. She didn't say, "Hasn't this been great?" Or, "Isn't this great?" She said, "Oh, Daddy, wouldn't this have been great?" Alex meant her whole life, if only she hadn't been sick.

I just said, "Yes," and after we hugged each other, she left the room, because, I knew, she wanted to let me cry alone. Alex knew by then that, if I cried in front of her, I would worry about upsetting her, and she didn't want to burden me that way. She was the only one dying.

CHAPTER 2

So we do have a few words of Alex's left, preserved on tape. And I remember very well, too, the last words Alex spoke. She said, "I love you, Chris," when her brother came into her room to say good-bye to her. After that, after Chris left, Alex was too exhausted even to whisper and only talked to Carol and me with her eyes.

Actually, too, she didn't quite say, "I love you, Chris"; as always, she said, "I love you, Chrish." This is what she called her brother. Say it out loud, and you will see why. If you say "Christopher"—which is what most people called Chris are officially named—there is a solid break between the "Chris-" and the "topher." But our Chris is a Christian, and going from the "Chris-" to the "-tian" requires the bridge of an *sh* sound, so that spelled phonetically, it is more properly *Chrishtian,* and therefore, in the diminutive, it really should be *Chrish.*

Alex started calling her brother that when she was about four years old. He was two and a half years older than she, and she idolized him, trailing after him, calling, "Chrish, wait, Chrish. . . ." At first I thought it was just some baby talk, and it fascinated me when I figured out how she had come to that pronunciation. It is an insignificant thing, to be sure, but I point it out to show that Alex really did have the most

11

incredible ear, as well as a gift for mimicry to go with it. My mother is from Virginia, and once, after visiting my parents for a few days, Alex came back with an absolutely perfect southern accent. I know just about anybody can manage a "y'all" and get by, but Alex was much more sophisticated; she caught the subtle inflections—"myarket" she would say, for that place where southerners go to buy food—and even the distinctive body movements that go with the dialect.

There was always an irony to Alex. She was, on the one hand, utterly vulnerable, helpless against this disease that was destroying her day by day, and yet she was, often, quite cool—even professional, I would say—in the way she conducted herself as a patient, as a victim. If she must be a victim, then she would be good at that. This is what made it so much harder for Carol and me, even as it made us prouder. Of all the people surrounding Alex, none played a role in the drama of her dying nearly so well as she played hers. And hers, of course, was the most difficult. Imagine knowing how, as a child, to go about dying. She never made any mistakes in that line. And it was, assuredly, not a matter of innocence either.

Her doctor, Tom Dolan, used to say that Alex was "seven, going on twenty-eight," and often with grownups a very discernible part of her made her their peer. I don't mean she was some woman-child, like a growing girl on the cusp of maturity who is never quite sure where she stands. Not that; but, uncannily, Alex always understood that something in her was already a woman, and she became what she had to be in the proper place. I think some of this came simply from being around adults more than other children, because she was so often in the hospital. But I think some of it was her secret, too. Alex sensed that she was going to die long before she truly understood it, and that made her special. Perhaps just that is what put her closer to God. I don't know.

Sometimes, when I went out with Alex, just the two of us, I really felt as if I was going along with a little person, a contemporary. In comparable circumstances with Chris, even though we might have more in common—two guys going to a ball game or something—no matter what, I always knew I was with my son. Alex mixed things up. She even took to calling me "my little Daddy" the last couple years. There was nothing rational in that—I'm not even physically little— but sometimes I thought it was really quite apt, that I was more her little thing than she mine.

People ask me, how can you do this, write about her, go through the anguish all over again? And that is a fair question. I am so sick of crying. It goes on and on. And it's strange in a way, because I thought I managed very well at the end. Why, it was supposed to be so difficult, but nobody ever told me quite how easy dying is, when it isn't you dying. No, the trouble is more afterward; it's the missing that's so hard. And this makes me miss Alex all the more, sifting through the drawings, seeing her face in the photographs, seeing her move on the screen, reading the things she wrote or people wrote about her, listening to her on tape. *Pass the soap, Mom!*

Of course, it hurts when anyone you love dies. But when it is a child who dies—when it is your child—as the grief fades naturally, there still remains that vacuum, and it is re- placed by anger. More fury is growing within me that Alex never had her fair chance. I didn't have time to be mad when she was dying; there was no room for that then. But now . . .

Then, too, the trouble with people who give so much, as Alex did, is that when they leave you there is so much more that they take away with themselves. And what makes it hard- est of all with Alex is that she was so extraordinary, so special, that she has become a sort of ideal for me. Believe me, this is not just some sad and biased father talking. The teacher who was my adviser in high school, A. J. Downs, wrote me after she died: "Before we got too smart for our own good, we called people like Alex saints." Imagine yourself trying to live up to an eight-year-old child. It's very disorienting.

Cyd Slotoroff is a young woman, a pediatric music specialist, who entertained the children in the ward at Yale–New Haven Hospital, where Alex spent so much time. Cyd played the guitar and sang along, doing many of her own songs. She symbolizes many of the adults with whom Alex became friends. Cyd says:

"I would feel selfish when I'd come to the ward and spend so much time alone with Alex. It wasn't only that she was my favorite child; it was just that there was no place else I'd rather be than with her. Alex was inspiring. I always felt honored just to be in her presence. Why couldn't we all be this way? She was so full inside, felt things so deeply, and she really came to affect my life. She was the most extraordinary child I ever met." Cyd stopped and paused.

"No, that's not quite right. You know that—Alex wasn't ever just a child. However old she was, she was just a human being.

"And more than that. You know, I never talked to Alex about God or anything religious, but she was the most spiritual person I ever met. I was driving along in my car—this was right after she died—and it was a beautiful clear day. The sky was so blue, and all of a sudden it seemed as if Alex's presence had expanded and filled everything. She had been released. I'd never felt anything like that before, any time in my life.

"God, what a blessing that child was! What a gift!"

And sometimes it is something like that for me, too. I say, *I'm sorry I did that, Alex.* Or, *I'm sorry I can't be as good as you, Alex.* Or sometimes I think, *What would Alex want me to do here?* What would she expect me to do? It frightens me most that I will meet some great test in my life—maybe one *for* my life, as she did—and I will not be able to do as well as my little baby girl did.

CHAPTER 3

For a few months there, right after Alex was born, I thought I had just about everything a man could want, at least in a textbook kind of way. I thought surely somebody from either the Census Bureau or the Department of American Dreams was going to get wind of me and come by and take publicity pictures. I had a job I loved, a career, a future, a house in the suburbs, and a VW bug and Ford Country Squire station wagon. I had a fluffy white dog named Chaucer who could sit up and beg, and a color television set that got good reception—eight VHF channels. I had a beautiful wife and a handsome, bright little son and heir, and then, a daughter, too. At the least, I thought someone should bring out a souvenir deck of cards featuring us, with a picture of the station wagon on one card, the dog sitting up and begging on another, me on a face card (probably the king of hearts), and so on.

Alex was the icing on the cake. Imagine getting your boy and your girl, just like that, in that order, exactly like in the comic strips. For a variety of reasons, everybody in the family especially wanted a girl, too. There hadn't been a female born in the Deford family in sixty-seven years, not since 1904. I was one of three brothers; I'd never even had a little girl around the house. And after I got my pal, Chris, Carol so

Carol with our baby daughter Alex, soon after her birth.

much wanted a daughter to fuss over and dress up and talk to. She was ecstatic when Alex was born.

That was October 30, 1971, shortly after dawn broke. They came out and told me that I had a fine, healthy daughter. I jotted it down in the margin of the page in the magazine that I was reading over and over; blue eyes; nineteen and a half inches long; five pounds, ten and three-fourths ounces. Alex had the same color eyes as her brother—although they would change to brown as she grew older—and she was only a half inch shorter than he had been, but, curiously, she weighed almost two pounds less than Chris had. Siblings usually weigh in about the same, so the disparity probably should have alerted someone. But it didn't. She just seemed a fine, healthy girl.

Only she wasn't. Alex was, right from the start, sick all the time. She ate voraciously, but food went right through her and she couldn't put on any weight. Besides, she always seemed to have colds and ear infections. But I didn't take it very seriously. The hospital had certified her healthy, so, certainly, nothing could be terribly wrong. The pediatrician finally said it was "failure to thrive," but even that didn't alarm me. I'd never been sick in my life, never been hospitalized except to have my tonsils out, and probably, deep inside, I harbored some intolerance against sick people. The way I saw it, Alex was probably just a slow learner at health, the way some kids are later at walking or talking.

Carol, however, grew increasingly worried; as the weeks went along, she could not ignore the fact that the baby just never seemed to come around, never quite got right, even though there wasn't one thing you could put your finger on. At that time, too, we both set a lot more store in hospitals and doctors. Then, on Washington's birthday, 1972, when Alex was almost four months old, Carol's father had a stroke and died. The day he was buried it snowed and was bitter cold, and when we returned from the funeral, the woman who had kept Alex for the day told us she was truly concerned about the baby. Alex was horribly pale, her eyes blank. Even to me, it was obvious she had never been so sick, so we went directly to the emergency ward of the nearest hospital, in Danbury. The doctor on duty examined Alex and said she certainly did have herself a little cold. He gave us a prescription that cost $1.69. I remember that very well. Even in 1972 I didn't know there were any prescribed medicines in existence that only cost $1.69.

That, as much as anything, assured us that Alex was going to be fine in another day or two.

But the next day, even with the $1.69 wonder drug, she grew worse. Luckily, by then Carol had begun to question the infallibility of medical personnel. It would take me a while longer. Carol took Alex to her regular pediatrician, and this time he diagnosed a serious case of double pneumonia and immediately admitted her to Danbury Hospital. One of the doctors who examined her there thought she showed the classic symptoms of cystic fibrosis and decided to test for that. Since 1953 there has been a special examination for the disease, which is known as "the sweat test," and while we were waiting for the results, I went to the encyclopedia and read about this cystic fibrosis. To me, at that point, it was one of those vague diseases you hear about now and then, sounding like some kind of clinging vine or a guy who kicks field goals with the side of his foot for the Kansas City Chiefs. I was very glad when the sweat test came back indisputably negative, because I had read that cystic fibrosis was fatal. Of course, I was not all that surprised; certainly no child of mine was going to have a fatal disease.

Then, after the weekend—hospitals just limp along on weekends, like the peacetime army or railroads—the hospital got around to doing all sorts of other tests on Alex. Soon enough, though, it was apparent that the doctors were really just fishing around. One day they were checking kidneys, the next day the brain.

It was Carol who finally had the good sense to say, "Frank, we've got to get Alex out of here." Carol is the one with the wise head in the family, although most people might not immediately appreciate this inasmuch as she is so pretty. She is a dead ringer for the actress Linda Evans, who was the star of *Dynasty*, one of those prime-time soap operas where everybody is devious and scheming. But Carol's character is not at all that of Linda Evans's TV milieu. She is clever, but direct.

For example, the first time I met Carol was at a college party weekend when I tried to pick her up. Somebody said to me that there was a pretty girl downstairs who had just broken up with her date, and was therefore obviously vulnerable with despair. However, Carol would have absolutely nothing to do with me, and, instead, chose a much more reliable and well-intentioned substitute escort for the weekend. A few years later, when we chanced to meet again, I dismissed this episode as (obviously) a mere passing instance of good judgment triumphing over natural instinct.

At Danbury, too, when she first told me that we must take Alex to another hospital, my initial response was that she was overreacting. "*They Are Doing Everything They Possibly Can,*" I said. And I'm sure they were, too. Only, of course, that wasn't the point. The trouble is, especially if you've never been sick yourself, it's awfully easy to maintain great faith in hospitals. This is particularly true nowadays, I guess, when so many other institutions are crumbling all around us. I always wanted to believe in hospitals; surely there are no doctors' dilemmas. And it is also true that with all Alex's hospitalizations I came to love some doctors and some nurses very much. But I learned this, too: You must guard against being hasty and promiscuous in the way you love medical people. Because some of them may hurt you. They will.

As a rule of thumb, whenever a doctor introduces himself as Doctor, but calls you by your first name, as if you were a child, be very wary. Carol learned to counter this by always trying to find out a doctor's first name. Then, if he smiled at her and said, "Carol, I'm Dr. Jones," she could reply, "Hello, Nick, I'm Mrs. Deford."

As for hospitals, there are four basic things you must understand.

1. You need to know your social security number.

2. Even if you have mastered number one, the accounting department is going to bill you incorrectly and then blame you. Whenever anything went wrong with Alex's treatment, I would think to myself, well, it could be worse, the doctors could have the batting average of the billing clerks— if that were so, every patient in the hospital would be graveyard dead.

3. You have to use one word all the time. That word is "why?" No matter what anybody in a hospital tells you—and especially if it involves your child—ask them why. Most doctors have a good bedside manner, but then, they're the bosses. When you confront them, especially standing up, eye to eye, they are not all that commanding; they are not any good at dissembling then, or even at hedging. Very few people dare ask doctors why. You'd be surprised; most always you can tell when a doctor is gilding the lily, or plain just doesn't know. Even Alex could spot the phonies by the time she was only six or seven. So ask why, and if that doesn't obtain satisfaction, ask why again. You will never regret it.

4. The elevators take forever.

We took Alex out of Danbury Hospital. Since she had defied diagnosis, we decided we had to go to the place everybody recommended, Children's Hospital in Boston. Even then, in 1972, Arabs were taking their children there. My uncle, who was a physician in Hartford, knew the chief of staff at Children's and made the arrangements. The volunteer fire department in the little town where we lived then—Redding, Connecticut—took Alex and Carol up in the town ambulance, for free. I drove to Boston, stopping in Rhode Island to drop Chris off with Carol's sister, his Aunt Gail. He was still a couple months short of his third birthday, couldn't appreciate the distressing situation, and, in fact, rather enjoyed the adventure of a visit to his cousins.

Everything was finally getting all straightened out. It was under control. Alex was going to get the medicine she needed for whatever she had and be just fine, ever after.

And, in fact, by the time I arrived at Children's, she had already been diagnosed.

She had cystic fibrosis.

There was no question. She had it. She had cystic fibrosis. They had just botched the sweat test at Danbury.

So, there it was. And things were moving very fast. The doctor called us into his office, and, after some consoling small talk, he spoke very frankly. I appreciated that. He told us he was sorry, but Alex would surely not live more than a few more days.

"There is no chance?" Carol asked.

"Yes, some. But very little. I don't want to mislead you," he said. "If by some . . . miracle, your baby is able to survive this crisis, I'm afraid that so much damage has been done to her lungs—so much deterioration—that we could never expect any sort of real recovery. At best, then, I don't believe she can live beyond two years."

He paused and let that sink in. Neither Carol nor I said anything; there wasn't anything to say. That was that.

Then the doctor leaned back in his chair. He wasn't just thinking. I could see that he was trying to decide whether or not he should tell us something. After a while, he decided he would, and he brought himself forward again, closer. "I know you don't know me," he began, "but this may be some consolation. My wife and I lost a child once, too. And she gave us a great deal of love and joy before she died, and that made it much harder for us. But the point is: We survived. We went on. You see—I'm here. And you'll go on, too. It'll be horrible. But you will overcome this."

We thanked the doctor for those words, but, at the moment, I don't think they registered. It was only with time that I came to understand them, and appreciate them. There was, however, something symbolic about that encounter, because, as the years passed, I was surprised to learn how many parents have lost children. There are more than you would imagine. But they are something of an underground, and you don't hear much about them, I guess, unless you find yourself in the same situation.

I think many of us have convinced ourselves that children don't die anymore, not in the latter half of the twentieth century, not in the United States of America, and certainly not in the suburbs. No, never in the suburbs. But some children still do die, despite what we tell ourselves, and this makes it all the more confounding for us when an Alex confronts us with her dying and her death. It is almost as if she had no business doing that to us.

CHAPTER 4

The doctor asked us next how we felt about keeping Alex alive if all hope ran out, if it were merely a matter of prolonging physical life. This was not difficult for us to deal with; neither of us wanted her kept alive without purpose. Besides, I think I had already begun to think of Alex as being dead.

There just didn't seem to be any other attitude to fall back on—safely, anyway. Alex was so sick, and also, I was so frightened. Here she was—this hideous, scrawny little mess. Her eyes filled up her whole face, and even then, going into her fifth month of life, she weighed barely a pound more than she had when she was born. There was nothing there, no place even for them to stick the needles. Finally, in desperation, they did find one vein they thought they could use. It was on her head, though, and the only way they could hold the IV in was by taping a paper cup from the cafeteria to her shaven skull. Somehow, this held the needle. It also gave Alex a crazy resemblance to that little kid in the old Coca-Cola advertisements, the one who wore a bottle cap for a hat.

I didn't know Alex yet. She was still so young, and, of course, she had always been sick. I guess that was the blessing. What frightened me was that she *would* survive this, and then I would get to know her, and then, then she would die and hurt me. That scared me more than the possibility that she might die immediately. I remember lying in the bed next to Carol that night, talking about this, about what we would do if Alex died. That would be God's will. If she lived to die some other time, it would be my distress. I fell off to sleep, praying that God's will be done.

In the next couple days, Alex did not do what she was supposed to—she did not die. In fact, she stabilized to the point that they moved her off the aisle. In the infants' ward the cribs are moved around all the time, with the most critical cases placed on the aisle, where they could be best monitored. When Alex had first come in, after the sweat test, they had put her on the aisle, right in the center of things, but then, after a few days when she did not die, they moved her down the row a crib or two.

We would come by and stare at her. She would stare back, and I assume she recognized us. Once I said, out loud, "Alex, are you going to die?" She didn't look any better. She was still this scarecrow of a child, seven pounds of bones, but for the first time it seemed that there was some shadow of expression on her face. It was not only a mask of pain and doubt.

A couple days later, when I came to the hospital first thing in the morning, Alex's crib had been moved back to the aisle. She didn't look any worse—the IV was still sticking out of her head, taped onto that crazy brown cafeteria cup—but I knew something must have gone wrong, or they wouldn't have moved her back out to the aisle.

The nurse came by then. She was the first of many I learned to appreciate. I said, "Miss Sarr, What's the matter with Alex now?"

"Oh, nothing, Mr. Deford," she replied, and rather gaily.

"But you've moved Alex back here, back out to the aisle."

"I must tell you about that," she said. "A couple of the other nurses and I were comparing notes, and we all agreed that there was something special about your baby." She looked down at Alex and smiled. Alex seemed to be looking back, checking things out. "As sick as Alex is, we discovered that she really didn't like it when we moved her crib off the aisle and down the row. She obviously liked it much better right here, where she could see everybody walking by, be right in the middle of all the activity. Her condition really started to decline when we moved her over there. So last night we decided we better get her back here, on the aisle, and she's much better now."

I was struck dumb. When Miss Sarr moved on, I cried for Alex—for *her*—for the first time. Oh, I'd cried before about this. I'm one of those people who cry all the time. I cry at weddings. I cry when people lose on TV quiz shows. I cry when people win on TV quiz shows. But I had never actually cried for Alex before, for her chances. But then . . . to understand that this little thing cared that much for life, even if she didn't know anything for certain about it except that it hurt all the time. From then on I wanted her to live, because Alex had become a whole, real person.

I never let myself hide behind God's will again either. Other things of God's were suddenly more important to me: I wanted so much for Alex to see flowers. I don't know why this mattered all of a sudden, but it did. When she was born, at the end of October, all the flowers were gone, and it just didn't seem right that she should die before she ever saw anything bright and fine and lovely, instead of the inside of a crib, the dark and cold of winter, and needles and pain.

A couple days later I went back home and tried to start up a working life again. Chris stayed in Rhode Island, and Carol moved in with her cousin Jane in Boston. In Redding it was just me and the dog, Chaucer, who could sit up and beg. It was still bitter cold, but oil was not a big deal then, so I turned up the heat and lit a fire to boot, fed Chaucer, had a couple of bourbons, and then wrote a letter. It said:

March 6, 1972

Dear Alexandra,

I write this for myself, really, and not to you, but for you and me both.

Someday, years from now, I will give you this—perhaps when you marry or when you have your first child.

It is late now, and I am tired. I just came back here, to your first home, in Redding, Connecticut, from Boston, where you are still in the hospital, and where they say you might yet die. But if I can pray for one thing in my life, it is that you will be back here soon, before spring comes, and then you will grow up here with us, and you will grow up smart and clever and pretty and happy, and strong and healthy, too.

You must see spring, Alex. And the next spring, and the one after. And you will always have the advantage over everyone else because each spring will be more glorious to you because each spring will find you better.

And one best spring, when the cold goes away, and the wind blows over the fresh green grass, and the robins bring our dreams back, then you will be well. And then you and I will walk on the clover and peer through the dogwood back to 1972, and laugh together that ever I worried that you might not come home, and grow up.

Of course, then springs won't mean nearly so much to you because you'll just take them

26

for granted, like everybody else. Oh well, you can't have everything.

Alex, I guess I'll be somewhere in my fifties when I give you this. Either that or I'll be gone and your mother will find this and give it to you for me. Either way, I want you to know that that will be my happiest moment ever.

I look at you now, and I see those big round blue eyes of yours staring back at me, wondering, asking, hurting, and I think you know more than you let on. Already you possess things I've never had, because you have had to struggle to earn life. And soon you'll have a spring, too.

Well, thanks for everything. You've already given me so much, and you must get well to help me grow better, with you. I want so much to get to know you. Now Chaucer and I will go to sleep. God bless you always, Alex.

With love,
Your father

I put that in an envelope, addressed it to Alex, and put a stamp on it. Eight cents. Then, across the stamp in the manner of a postmark, I wrote the year, 1972, in orange grease pencil, and, the next day, I put the envelope in the safe deposit box, where it has stayed until now.

At the time, I firmly believed that Alex would be cured and would get to read the letter. I believed that with all my heart.

CHAPTER 2

CHAPTER 5

The next few years were nearly beautiful. What was different and difficult about Alex because of her disease was papered over by our dreams. She did not know yet about dying, and did not have to give any time or thought to that. Why, we were almost like any family, Alex almost like any child. Apparently, we were nearly as perfect as those families Alex began to meet on television—*The Brady Bunch*, *The Partridge Family*, *I Love Lucy* reruns, *Happy Days*—where nobody ever gets sick. People in television families get pregnant and beat up, they get mixed up and insulted, they're not invited to the prom. But they never get sick. It is against the law for anyone in a television family to get sick.

In many ways our life may have been its fullest during this period. It may yet be better, but it can never be so full again. You see, just as Alex did, we had to keep working for her life, sacrificing, enduring the ritual of her treatments every day. But that time and effort was easy to give then, easy to justify, because she did get better, and she stayed better. Her success was so obvious that the blind faith I held for her future mellowed into a real trust. In the summer of 1974, when we moved to a new house, about twenty miles away, in Westport, down by Long Island Sound, I wrote this to myself: "From everything I know at this time, I expect Alex can live a fairly normal life in this house until she is ready to leave it some day when she is grown."

That was the house she would die in, before she finished third grade.

But, oh, I wish you could have seen her then, before the disease took her apart. What a little beauty Alex was.

So much is abnormal about a child dying; it threatens the simple, normal rhythm of life. For example, I knew cystic fibrosis was a progressive disease. I knew that, and you could sit there and tell me cystic fibrosis was a progressive disease until you were blue in the face, but how could a rational grown man ever contemplate that that beautiful child before him would deteriorate while her contemporaries matured and blossomed?

I wasn't ignorant, either. I had been elected to the national board of the Cystic Fibrosis Foundation. I knew what the score was. I knew there wasn't some kindly old doctor in a smock, mixing beakers and vials, just about ready to say, "Eureka!" And then, "Take two of these before bedtime for a week, and your cystic fibrosis will be cured by next Tuesday." I knew that wasn't in the cards. I knew how bad it could be. We trustees met twice a year, the first weekends in May and December. There was hardly a period between meetings when we didn't get a message from the president, Doris Tulcin, saying, sorry, but so-and-so, our fellow trustee, has lost a child. One trustee lost his only two children between meetings.

But no matter how much I knew and how many other children died, I would never admit that it could be my child sometime. It must be just like that in battle on the front lines.

It was easy to be deluded, too, because Alex did appear so healthy for a while. She was so pretty, and she was all but free of pain. The pneumonia and the ear problems had all been cleared up, and the medicines and physical maintenance techniques kept her protected.

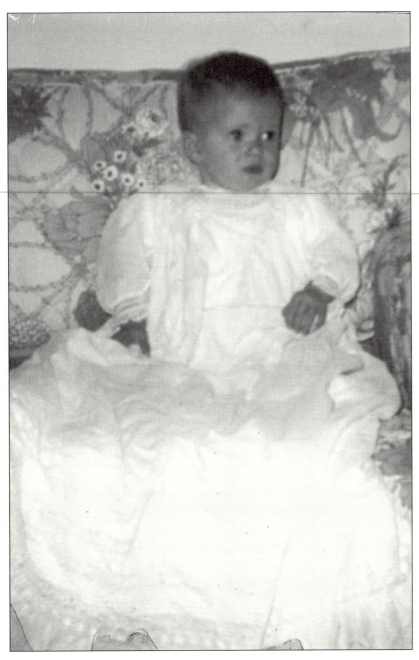

Alex's christening picture in 1972, only months after she'd been all but given up for dead.

Soon Alex was downright fat, and when at last her hair began to grow out from where it had been shaved off for the IVs on her head, she started looking healthier than the rest of us. We're all skinny. Carol had been a model, that skinny, and Chris is painfully thin, such a picky eater that he can tell margarines apart in taste tests and refuses to touch all but one brand. But Alex—as soon as she woke up in the morning, she was ready to chow down, and by the time she was christened in the fall of '72, just short of her first birthday, she was chubby; with her burr haircut she looked not unlike some kind of baby-faced punk rocker.

Oh, I wish you could have seen her then. She was christened in a long white gown of lace that had been in my mother's family for generations. Her blue eyes had already turned to brown, which fit her better, matched her hair. She grew even more beautiful in the next couple years, taking on an almost eerie resemblance to the photographs of her mother as a baby.

Alex knew that, too. She knew she was pretty, the way all pretty girls know they're pretty. But she wasn't any coy or fragile belle. True enough, she wasn't at all athletic (and, I'm sure, wouldn't have been even if she had been healthy), but she was always lively, and no one was ever more animated. Alex always wanted to be up and doing something. I filmed one wonderful moment, so typical of her, when Chris got off the school bus his first day back from kindergarten. Alex, who was not quite three at the time, was there to greet him. All of a sudden, as Chris comes down the steps, Alex springs to life and starts slapping his palms, as if he were just coming into the dugout after blasting a home run. Now where in the world did she get that? Turn the camera on Alex and she would *do* something; dance, curtsy, clap, blow kisses, whatever, some action.

She grew up exceptionally feminine, but not in the old-fashioned way; she was a feminine feminist. No one ever liked silly frilly things as much as Alex did. The more gossamer, the better. She couldn't abide pants—too masculine—even when it was bitter cold. Alex fibbed, like any child, but the only time I ever recall contrived, premeditated, real A-1 lies came in nursery school when she advised Carol that the teacher wanted her to wear dresses to school, and then turned around and told the teacher that her mother would not allow her to wear pants to school—no matter how cold it was.

Alex was heavy into cosmetics when she was hardly out of diapers, and you could usually hear her coming, rattling like Marley's ghost with all the cheap jewelry that clanked about her. Alex would have killed for jewelry. We would bury her with a lot of her favorite jewelry.

Earrings were her favorites. One day, when she was about five or six, Alex and Carol went out shopping to a store with a going-out-of-business sale. Alex's eyes were drawn to a pair of the ugliest earrings you ever did see. It was not enough that they were hideous. They were huge, hanging down to the poor wearer's shoulder, and they glimmered, drawing further attention. Not only that, but they didn't come cheap. Even 50 percent off, going-out-of-business, they were still commanding $12.50, plus tax. "Please, Mother, please," Alex pleaded.

Carol patiently showed Alex that the earrings were simply too big. On Alex, they almost came to the waist. But she would not be denied. Hadn't Carol already made the mistake of saying that she adored them, too?

"You've got to get them for yourself, Mother."

"But they're too expensive," Carol said.

"Oh, don't worry, Mother. I'll talk to Daddy. I will. It'll be all right."

Carol was running out of excuses. "The trouble is, Alex," she said, "that these earrings are just so pretty, so magnificent, that I would never have the right occasion to wear them."

"Oh, yes you will," Alex said.

"When?" Carol asked.

"When they find the cure for cystic fibrosis and we have that big family party and get all dressed up—you can wear them then."

Carol bit the tears back and said of course and bought the earrings. They're still in a drawer.

Makeup was as much an obsession as jewelry for Alex. As she grew older and got more sophisticated with her drawings, for example, every face had to have two big red circles on the cheeks—rouge. My favorite drawing of hers said:

Happy Valentin Day   God   Love Alex

With it there were renderings of the obligatory heart, rainbow, and lollipop flower and the word *God,* with an arrow pointing to a large, smiling face. And this face had two red dots for rouge on the cheeks. Only Alex would put God in makeup.

But although I never heard Alex directly suggest that God was a woman, I wouldn't be surprised if she had believed it. Alex instinctively believed in women, and believed they got a raw deal. From an early age, and without any prompting, she questioned why there were no women this or no women that. "Where are the girls?" she would say. "Why aren't there any ladies?" On *Star Trek,* she strictly concerned herself with Lieutenant Uhura, and on *Captain Kangaroo* with Debbie (good choice: I had a crush on Debbie, too). Instead of the male superheroes, Alex inclined to the likes of Wonder Woman, the Bionic Woman, and Isis. Unlike a lot of little girls, Alex never had much interest in horses—not until the great filly Ruffian came along and Alex started hearing that she could beat the colts, the boy horses. Alex wasn't the least bit impressed that I was off to cover the Olympics in 1976 until Nadia Comaneci suddenly started making perfect scores and stealing all the thunder from male athletes.

I want to guard against reading significance into everything about Alex, but I do believe that her almost instinctive feminism came out of some greater sense she had to detect the unfairness of life. *Wouldn't this have been great?* Next to love itself, equality and beauty were the things that interested her the most.

Alex was an idealist, a revolutionary. But she was also a distinct, even shameless, flirt. I'd always heard that little girls are supposed to have special relationships with their fathers, and while Carol and Alex were, as mother and daughter, close in ways I could never begin to fathom, there was no question but that Alex knew how to handle me. From the time she was only two or three, she could do extraordinary imitations of the sexpots she saw on television. She could slink better than any four-year-old I ever saw, and before long she started throwing out her chest—although getting a little mixed up verbally as she did so. Alex referred to breasts as *hips*, obviously confusing the word with a fairly similar four-letter slang term for breasts, which she must have heard somewhere along the way (although surely never around our house, from the lips of her sainted father).

Alex was a physically affectionate child, too, one who loved to touch, to cuddle, to hug and kiss, to give and receive back rubs. Her kissing even got a little embarrassing for a while; she went through a stage when she offered up wet, sloppy, open-mouthed ones. Responsibility for that went to Chris, because he had advised Alex, "That's how teenagers kiss." Mercifully, that fancy passed soon enough and we got back to more standard kissing. Best of all, though, Alex just liked to get all gussied up in a long, fancy gown, with lots of jewelry and globs of makeup, and sit close to me, her date.

She knew how to make a guy jealous, though. She would let me know that her *real* boyfriends were (depending on her mood and television scheduling) Don Ho, Donny Osmond, and Bobby Vinton. For a couple years, Mr. Vinton had a show that originated, for some reason, in Toronto. It was broadcast every Tuesday night at 7:30 on our local channel, and it was the focus of Alex's—and the family's—week. When we would tuck her in, I would tell Alex tales of the times I had actually been to Toronto, and she would fall asleep, a smile on her face, dreaming of this glorious Shangri-La by Lake Ontario from whence cometh Bobby Vinton, face and music. She was so happy, so pretty, and for just that brief time, there was hardly any pain. Oh, I wish you could have seen her then.

CHAPTER 6

One of the reasons I find it difficult sometimes to comprehend quite all that Alex meant to other people—especially to those who only met her nearer the end—is that, much as I loved her, proud as I was of her, I always knew her as a little person, a child, a very fallible human being. Alex could be petulant and cross, and, especially early on, when she was relatively at her healthiest, she was inclined to take things too seriously, too literally, and show little humor. The Halloween of '74, the day after her third birthday, she dressed up as bossy Lucy, from "Peanuts," and we all laughed at Alex because we thought the casting was so apt. She didn't get the joke.

That was the time in her life when Alex looked and felt her best. But even then we never had the luxury of being able to close our eyes and pretend. When a child has cystic fibrosis, she never simply lives. She must be kept alive. It's a lot of work, too. Even now, long after Alex has gone, I wake up some mornings with a vague feeling that something is incomplete in my life, that there is some obligation I've forgotten.

Even now it seems strange for me and for the family just to get up, brush our teeth, put on our clothes, eat breakfast, and go on about the business of another day of living. Because when Alex was with us, even when she was doing pretty well, we had to go through lengthy, set routines every day just to help her live. And after you've done that for a while, after helping to keep someone living has become part of the rhythm of your existence, then merely getting up again in the morning and accepting life—no questions, no effort— can be very flat, even disorienting.

Some diseases, even some fatal ones, don't put too many demands on the family of the patient. But cystic fibrosis is a tyrant that rules everyone in the family. There is no avoiding it; it is at once clinging and creepy, smothering and penetrating; maddening for sure; often it can destroy the whole family, even as it takes the one child's life.

Cystic fibrosis utterly defies a cure. It is a genetic disease, carried almost exclusively by Caucasians, but with little fluctuation in incidence anywhere in the white world. Apparently it's been with us from antiquity. Cystic fibrosis patients give off an excess of salt; this is reflected in a German folk saying: "The baby who is kissed at birth and tastes salty will have a short life."

One out of every twenty whites carries the defective gene, as I do, as Carol does, as perhaps ten million other Americans do—a population about the size of Illinois or Ohio. Indeed, the CF gene is so prevalent that one of my colleagues at the foundation, Dr. Charles Lobeck, even speculates that at some point in human development the defect served a necessary—even beneficial—purpose. But carriers, the tens of millions of us in the world, are unmarked in any way, and no carrier has any way of knowing that he is a carrier until he marries another carrier who has no way of knowing that she is a carrier until they have a baby who is diagnosed with CF. Research into carrier identification does appear to be well along the path to success, and it is reasonable to expect that an effective and fairly inexpensive test may be ready within the next few years, but as yet one does not exist. If Carol and I had been lucky, if our second-born had not been cursed with cystic fibrosis, then we probably never would have had another child, and our bad genes would merely have been passed on, blissfully unknown to us.

The laws of genetics are pretty unyielding, of course. One out of every four children born to two carriers will have the disease. One out of four will be free and clear. The other two will be carriers. But it's like flipping coins. There is no reason for the unlucky ones to pop up in the order that they do. Surely, many undiagnosed CF carriers have numerous children, none afflicted. Similarly, others have a sick child right away, their firstborn. And some of these parents, by ignorance or design, go on having babies. Many families have two CF kids, a few even three or more.

Carol and I never even considered trying to have another child. If you're carriers, you can get better odds, of 5-1, playing Russian roulette than the 3-1 cystic fibrosis offers you at life. But I must say this: Had Alex died at Children's, as she was supposed to, Carol and I would never have known what hell cystic fibrosis truly is, and maybe, in that ignorance, we would have decided to take the 3-1 and gamble. I think that is possible, because although you may understand, intellectually, that cystic fibrosis is painful, fatal, incurable, depressing, expensive, and altogether horrible, until you have lived with it you can never comprehend how impossible it is. For CF families the divorce rate is several times the national average, and the incidences of separation, alcoholism, desertion, wife beating, and so on are all comparably high. And the physically healthy siblings, no less than the parents, are often crippled in many emotional ways.

I was lucky, you could say; I only had my child die.

Even in the best of times, when Alex was younger, she required almost as much daily attention as she did later, on the verge of death. The care, the demands, are constant; all the worse that there is a Sisyphean quality to them. In those first years, too, on top of everything else, Alex had to sleep every night in a mist tent. She despised that, as well you can imagine. Mercifully, after a while the expert consensus shifted, and the doctors decided that such tents were of dubious merit. However much they may help, originally, in the strict medical sense, they probably do more damage psychologically. So at least then Alex was permitted to sleep like any child, without the stigma of a tent.

Not too long ago I was crawling around up in our attic, searching for some old chairs. There are no lights in the attic, and suddenly, behind some worthless, nostalgic debris, loomed an apparatus I did not immediately recognize, a ghostly superstructure reminiscent of some rotting ship's hulk grounded on a sandbar. I peered closer in the dark, and finally recognized that it was the frame for Alex's mist tent. I had shoved it up there, out of my sight, when it had been declared unnecessary.

Softly, then, alone, I began to cry, for I could see Alex there in her crib, as a baby, as any baby, curled up with a doll and her pink "blankie," looking so cheerful, so chubby, even (it seemed) . . . so healthy. Chris would usually be the one to get her, then, to flip off her mist machine, pull back the plastic covering, clouded and dewy by now, snatch her up, and bring her into our bed, where we could all four snuggle together, putting off the morning, and the day's first treatments.

Cystic fibrosis is, notwithstanding its name, a disease primarily of the lungs. It has nothing to do with cysts. It was not identified as a distinct clinical entity until the midthirties, and not until some years later was the full pathology comprehended. Inexplicably, the disease attacks not only the lungs but other disparate parts of the body: the pancreas, the major digestive organ; and, in males, the testes. So it undermines breathing, eating, reproduction—all of life itself.

40

Alex doing her inhalation therapy. It sure beat sleeping in a mist tent.

The common agent in all cases is mucus. The cystic fibrosis victim's body manufactures too much mucus, or the mucus is too thick, or both. So baffling is the disease that nobody knows for sure which basic factor is the issue. Whatever, the mucus obstructs the airflow in the lungs and clogs the pancreas and the testes. Adding to the perplexity is the fact that no two patients have the same history, except in the sense that CF is always progressive, always terminal.

The luckiest patients are those born without lung involvement. Others have such mild cases that they go undetected for years; quite possibly there are even some CF patients who never know they have the disease, but die relatively young of some misunderstood pulmonary involvement. At the other end of the spectrum, some infants are essentially born dead, their tiny bodies so ravaged by the disease that they cannot even begin to draw breath.

As events proved, Alex was toward the worse end of the spectrum. While she died at eight, half of the children now born in the United States with cystic fibrosis who are diagnosed and treated live to the age of eighteen. Be grateful for small favors. Back in the midfifties, when the Cystic Fibrosis Foundation was started, a child with CF could not even expect to live to kindergarten. Regrettably, early steady advances stopped just about the time Alex was born. Until the early seventies almost every passing year saw another year of life expectancy added for a CF kid, but these advances were somewhat illusory. They were largely prophylactic, stemming almost entirely from better maintenance and more powerful antibiotics. The longer life span in no way indicated an approaching cure, nor even a control (as, for example, insulin keeps diabetes under control). In a sense, it isn't accurate to say that we kept Alex alive—we merely postponed her dying.

Alex's day would start with an inhalation treatment that took several minutes. This was a powerful decongestant mist that she drew in from an inhaler to loosen the mucus that had settled in her lungs. Then, for a half hour or more, we would give her postural drainage treatment to accomplish the same ends physically. It is quite primitive, really, but all we had, the most effective weapon against the disease. Alex had to endure eleven different positions, each corresponding to a section of the lung, and Carol or I would pound away at her, thumping her chest, her back, her sides, palms cupped to better "catch" the mucus. Then, after each position, we would press hard about the lungs with our fingers, rolling them as we pushed on her in ways that were often more uncomfortable than the pounding.

Some positions Alex could do sitting up, others lying flat on our laps. But a full four of the eleven she had to endure nearly upside down, the blood rushing to her head, as I banged away on her little chest, pounding her, rattling her, trying somehow to shake loose that vile mucus that was trying to take her life away. One of her first full sentences was, "No, not the down ones now, Daddy."

Psychologists have found that almost any child with a chronic disease assumes that the illness is a punishment. Soon, the treatment itself blurs with the disease and becomes more punishment. Sick children have highly ambivalent feelings about their doctors, on the one hand hating them for the pain and suffering they inflict, on the other admiring them, wanting to grow up and be doctors. Wendy Braun and Aimee Spengler, Alex's best friends, told me after Alex died that whenever the three of them played doctors and nurses, Alex participated with enthusiasm, but when she played the doctor, it was always cancer she was seeking to cure. She could not bring herself to be a cystic fibrosis doctor. As much as she adored and trusted her specialist, Tom Dolan, she must have associated too much pain with him ever to want to *be* him.

In cystic fibrosis a child must transfer this attitude toward the parents, as well, for we were intimately and daily involved in the medical process. Imagine, if you will, that every

day of your child's life you forced medicines upon her, although they never seemed to do any good; you required her
to participate in uncomfortable regimens, which you super-
vised; and then, for thirty minutes or more, twice a day, you
turned her upside down and pounded on her. And this never
seemed to help either. I have been told that parents let their
self-conscious resentment of the illness surface during the
treatments, and I must face the fact that this was sometimes
surely true of me, too. In some moments I must have thought
that I was also being punished.

And say what you will, explain to me intellectually all
you want about how much the postural drainage helped
Alex—still, when every day I had to thump my little girl,
pound away on her body, sometimes when she was pleading
with me, crying out in pain to stop, something came over me,
changed me. I guess, over eight years, I did therapy two thousand times, and Carol many more, probably three thousand,
having to manage both times each day when I was traveling.
I never understood how she managed. But still, me: Two
thousand times I had to beat my sick child, make her hurt and
cry and plead—"No, not the down ones, Daddy"—and in the
end, for what?

After the therapy was finished, we had to start on the
medicines. I recall how exciting it was during one period—
Alex was two and a half—when she *only* had to take one antibiotic. How glorious that was, just one antibiotic every day.
Usually it was two, and Dr. Dolan had to keep changing
them, as Alex's body built up immunities.

She had to take many other medications, too, including, relentlessly, an enzyme preparation named Viokase. The
bulk of Viokase is animal enzyme, which Alex needed because
her pancreas couldn't produce sufficient enzymes of its own.
Relative to the medicines that dealt primarily with her lung
problems, Viokase was pretty effective. The minority of CF
patients who don't have lung involvement initially can get by

with the pancreas problem as long as they diligently take their enzyme substitutes. Alex had to take Viokase every time she ate anything. Of course, considering her lung condition, this seemed like small potatoes. Carol and I didn't even think about it much.

For most of her life, before she learned to swallow pills, Alex took the Viokase as a powder, mixed into applesauce, which was an inexpensive carrying agent that could transport the drug into the system without its breaking down. And so, before every meal she ever ate, Alex had a plate of applesauce with the enzyme powder mixed in. It was foul-tasting stuff, a bitter ordeal to endure at every meal. "Oh, my appasaws," she would moan, "my appasaws," always pronouncing it as if it were a cousin to chain saws or buzz saws.

"Come on, Alex, eat your Viokase," I would say, and rather impatiently, too. After all, she had already been through an inhalation treatment, a half hour of physical therapy, several liquid medications—so what was the big deal with the applesauce. *Come on, let's go.* Alex had had a great appetite when she was younger, but a few years later she'd just pick at her food. It occurred to me then that if all your life eating was a project, and you couldn't eat a lot of the delicious things everybody else enjoyed, eventually eating would bore you. Imagine having to start off with applesauce every time you ate anything—and not getting much sympathy for it, either.

Later, doctors and nurses or other people would say, "Alex seems to have lost her appetite," and I would nod gravely, being pretty sure by then that it was psychological. Eating, like everything else for Alex, had become strictly a matter of staying alive.

When she was very young, before she began to comprehend how pointless it all was, Alex was wonderfully accepting of all that was demanded of her. At first, like any baby, she wasn't in any position to quibble; she just seemed to go along, assuming that inhalation, applesauce, and all that were things all babies endured. When she played with her dolls, she would give them therapy, putting off the down ones if the dolls behaved. After a time Alex began to notice that her brother was not required to endure what she did every day, but that didn't bother her too much, either. Since she was the only baby girl around, she simply assumed that therapy was something that all babies and/or all girls must go through.

Only slowly did the recognition come that she was singled out for these things. Then she began to grope for the implications. One spring day when she was four, Alex came into my office and said she had a question. Just one was all she would bother me with. All right, I asked, what was it. And Alex said, "I won't have to do therapy when I'm a lady, will I?"

It was a leading question; she knew exactly where she was taking me.

As directly as I could I said, "No, Alex"—not because I would lie outright about it, but because I knew the score by then. I knew that she would not grow up to be a lady unless a cure were found.

CHAPTER 7

There must be, as I have heard, some instinct of death among those who are facing it—even if they have no real concept of what death might be. Apparently, a child does not possess the capacity to assess the future—let alone death—until puberty. Chris always seemed like a fairly average kid in this regard. Except perhaps for "Bang, bang, you're dead" while playing cowboys and Indians, the subject never seemed to enter his mind. But from an early age, even when Alex played by herself, death was a topic for her.

The metaphysical questions—What is death? Where do we go?—would come later, but death was always a part of things. For example, she would come to me and say, "Daddy, would you hold my doll? She's sad. She's crying."

"What's the matter with her, Alex?"

"She just heard that her grandmother died."

People were always dying in Alex's fantasies. It was a way of life for her.

The summer of 1975, when Alex was going on four, Ruffian, the great filly, had to be destroyed after she broke a leg in a match race against Foolish Pleasure, the champion colt, at Belmont Park. Alex took an exceptional amount of interest in the race, because Carol and I were going out to see it, because she could watch it herself on television at her

47

grandmother's, and because, as I mentioned, it was a matter of girl against boy.

When Ruffian had to be destroyed, Alex was heart-broken, and we spent a lot of time discussing the hereafter. Pretty much, though, we restricted this to horses: Would Ruffian be in our people heaven, or do animals have their own? In the years that followed, whenever the subject of horses would arise, Alex would bring up Ruffian. She had kept a photograph of the horse.

They buried Ruffian near the finish line at Belmont Park. Alex asked me to take her out there, and I said I would, but I never did. I had it all set once, but then she had to go back in the hospital, and somehow we just never got around to it after that. The two things I never took Alex to, that I meant to, were to see where Ruffian was buried, and to see a circus. I just never got around to them, and I hate myself for it to this day.

That, and I always forgot the damn flashbulbs.

The summer before, 1974, we had moved to West-port, and by chance this brought us closer to the cystic fibro-sis clinic in New Haven instead of the one in Hartford. Carol started taking Alex to Yale–New Haven Hospital for her regu-lar checkups. It was still only a matter of checkups. Alex hadn't been required to go back as an inpatient since infancy. And so, one day early in December of 1974, Carol took Alex up to Yale–New Haven for a regular appointment. Her new doctor was Tom Dolan. He is a Harvard man, a Red Sox fan, and a golfer, but, notwithstanding these constitutional deficiencies, I learned to put up with him.

Tom Dolan could no doubt be making a better living with more comfortable hours in private practice—and once he left the clinic and tried that—but he soon returned to Yale–New Haven and his young cystic fibrosis patients. I don't know how he does it. Nobody he takes care of ever gets well, and most of them die in his care. And it's not his fault, and they're children. It's a hard loaf for Tom Dolan—and for all the doctors like him. It was as easy to admire him as to like him.

Long before I had met Tom I had learned, at a foundation trustees meeting, that perhaps the worst thing about cystic fibrosis is that it attracts a bacteria known as pseudomonas. The excessive, filthy mucus overwhelms the defense mechanisms in the lungs, so the pseudomonas bacteria colonize there. Pseudomonas is most common with cystic fibrosis, but it is also a threat to patients who have been severely burned, and it is found in the bloodstreams of certain types of cancer patients. Still, for all the research that has been done, there is as yet no antibiotic to deal with pseudomonas, and once it begins to march through the lungs, it multiplies with impunity and sweeps everything in its path. For any cystic fibrosis patient, pseudomonas is the harbinger of death.

Carol came back from the checkup that day in December and told me Dr. Dolan said that Alex had this new thing in her lungs. Obviously, he had tried to put the best face on it, and I played altogether dumb. "What's that?" I said. "Pneumonia?"

"No, it's pseudomonia," Carol said, still not sure, and when she went on and told me what I already knew, that there were no antibiotics to combat it, I downplayed that news, too. We were usually pretty honest with each other, but this was one time I didn't see any sense in upsetting Carol any more than necessary. Just because I knew too much, why should she also have to hear the other shoe drop? She'd know soon enough.

I already did. I was puttering around my office a few days later when Alex came gaily skipping in, all dressed up. It was my birthday, my thirty-sixth, and we were going to have a family party. She was so happy, so pretty, and it destroyed me, because suddenly all I could notice was her fingers. It hadn't hit me before. They were starting to get clubbed from the disease. It was the first real outward and visible sign—there wasn't enough oxygen to reach the tips of the fingers—as sure as the pseudomonas was starting to ravage her in places we could not see.

So, on my birthday, I started to cry, and held her to me, and told her they were tears of happiness. She was young enough then to believe me; she still took the world at face value, as healthy kids do.

But it was, starting about that time, that Alex began to sense our apprehensions, her plight; somehow then, if only subconsciously, she began to understand that she might die, whatever that meant. More and more, death became a part of her. I remember, for example, an occasion about a year later when we all four went out to dinner at the Pancake House. Alex was really feeling her oats that evening, and at one point she went over to a table where a man was having dinner by himself. He had just finished his meal, and Alex carefully inspected his plate, just as her mother would hers—perfect mimicry. "Hmmm," Alex said then, imitating a mother, "you did a good job."

The man laughed heartily, as the waitress did, as we all did—except Chris, who, as the grown-up big brother, was mortified by the scene. Then Alex, encouraged by the critical acclaim for her act, paraded up to the cash register. There was another waitress there, with a cigarette, and Alex shook her head and said, "You know, you'll die if you don't stop smoking." Possibly, Alex had gone over the line; she wasn't cute anymore; she had grown fresh. But that's not the point: She spoke to the waitress in the same casual way, in the same friendly tone, as she had spoken to the customer. Somehow I felt she was purposely making the subject of death an easy, everyday part of her life.

Alex as Wonder Woman and Chris as . . . whatever . . . liven up one of our Halloweens.

And sometimes Alex would take it even deeper, and fall into blue periods, when the topic of death was not merely idle conversation, but where it took on real emotional impact. On those occasions, when Alex would play by herself, which she did often and well, her dolls would be suddenly faced with impending demise, or would already have gone on to their reward. Sometimes it was actual local acquaintances, she said, who had just "died."

Occasionally, too, Alex would bring us into the game as straight men. Putting on a long face, she would walk around, shaking her head, saying over and over, "Oh, I'm so sad, I'm so sad."

We had to bite. "Why, Alex?"

"Because both my great-grandmothers died six years ago."

That was all make-believe. The subject of great-grandmothers, all actually long deceased, certainly never came up. But it served Alex's purpose. In her own childish way she was being careful, even calculating, starting to face death. It was as if nature was somehow preparing her, while being careful to protect her, too. The blue periods never lasted for long—a couple of days at a stretch. They did not swirl down into any sustained morbidity. And never in these private sessions did Alex permit her imagination to go too far; never did Carol or Chris or I meet a pretend death—and certainly never Alex herself.

There was some sort of self-imposed taboo. Alex was testing herself, seeing how far she could go with the subject, knowing somehow that she must begin to deal with this business, but that she must never let it rule her. She would hold death at arm's length, where she could keep an eye on it. It was all quite extraordinary. Something within Alex began preparing her for her doom at approximately the same time that her body first really began to decline.

CHAPTER 8

She is an incurable child, God.

She has only a few years to live, unless a cure is found soon. In my weakest moments, I want to shout and cry out for you to work a miracle as I want it. But I know that your will and ways are beyond my understanding.

The child is created in your image, isn't she, Lord? This means that she possesses your dignity and beauty, your mystery and deep purpose. So, your healing and blessing are constantly at work in her soul, mind, and body. I am grateful that she came from you and will return to you, with perfect care. I thank you, God, that she rests in your arms.

Open my eyes to see the reality of your radiant love in her face. Let me see your victory in her trusting eyes.

A friend of mine, Malcolm Boyd, the Episcopal priest and author of *Are You Running with Me, Jesus?* and many other books, wrote that prayer for me when Alex was six. I read it at a trustees meeting. Once the pseudomonas was discovered, I began, in some way, to prepare myself for Alex's death. From a practical point of view I knew that I had to give up even hoping for a cure. I felt that a more sensible wish would be that an effective antibiotic against pseudomonas could be found, which would buy Alex more time, during which the actual cure or a control might be discovered. Even this, I came to learn, was wishful thinking, false optimism, for, as a doctor once told me, if pseudomonas could be conquered, the chances were pretty good—nature abhors a vacuum and all that—that yet another virus, potentially one even more damaging, more cunning, might well pop up in its stead.

It was all quite maddening. I had been genuinely optimistic in the beginning—especially after Alex recovered so magnificently at five months. Besides, even the most rational of us can believe in miracles that remain, safely, a tomorrow away. Also, even the most cynical of us can believe in them—can believe in anything—when we need to for our own child's life.

But, when it doesn't work out, when the miracle doesn't flash on the screen or jump out of the computer, when, on some tomorrow, your child dies instead, a lot of the child in you dies, too. I am not a nihilist or a sourpuss now that Alex is dead. I still laugh and love, marvel at the wonders of humanity and praise God for His. Neither, though, am I any wiser or stronger—and certainly no better—for what I went through. People assume you must be better for the experience, but I don't see why that must follow.

Neither must you necessarily abandon your faith. However, you do lose something every bit as important, for when your child dies, you yourself are robbed of that childish sanity that makes it tolerable to accept growing old. I don't see the incongruity of life so well anymore, because my child dying is the ultimate incongruity. A capricious world is much easier to deal with than the disordered one I have been forced to inhabit.

I do find one solace. Now that it is Alex who is dead (and not me), I really don't worry anymore about my own death. Oh sure, when the plane bumps about I gasp and grab the armrest and pray fervently that it will not plunge thirty-seven thousand feet and leave me in a number of charred little bits and pieces. I would not care for that at all. I'm not fey. But if you have an adorable little girl, and she up and dies, then a number of rules seem changed, including those of death itself. I can't be frightened to follow Alex, wherever to. I mean, first, strictly from a selfish point of view, dying is the only way I can possibly be with her again. But beyond that, Alex has, in her way, reduced all my normal maunderings about God and the hereafter to one terribly simple proposition. If there is a heaven—must be a heaven—great. If not, if this incredible little person spent eight years in pain, cursed, hopeless, only to completely disappear, poof, like that, then it is all quite pointless, all a gag, and it is of no great consequence to me whether or not I'm asked to participate in life as straight man or comic.

That is simplistic, I know. And I'm certainly aware that I'm not the first father to lose a child. I didn't discover death and capture it on the Betamax. But, all the same, subtleties do become elusive when you are caught in this situation. As I wrote to our minister after Alex died: "If there are no atheists in foxholes, neither do I think there can be any atheists among parents whose children die." In fact, because of Alex I'm sure that I'm a more religious person, more of a Christian, with stronger beliefs. And this has comforted me. But I'm also enough of a natural skeptic to suspect the integrity of my belief. Is my faith really stronger, or am I just talking myself into something in the hope that wishing makes it so . . . you now, foxhole-wise?

One thing, quite this side of faith, I am sure of. Alex herself showed me, changed me. I do feel differently now. Above all, I feel differently about differences. I came to appreciate these more because Alex was so unusual herself. When she coughed in public, I could see people glance over at her, disgusted, sure she was spreading germs. When Alex became so horribly skinny, I could see some strangers peering at her as at a curiosity, staring at her knees, which were set out like two huge lumps from her matchstick limbs. I came to love those strangers we passed who looked, and saw, and then moved on, naturally.

So perhaps I am better in one way: I am more tolerant. But that is not because Alex died; that is because of the way she lived. Once you have gone somewhere in public—anywhere, and only once is necessary—and you realize that people are looking at your child, finding her grotesque or disgusting in whatever way—that she is too skinny or her fingers are clubbed and funny shaped or she coughs or gasps—once you have experienced that, you really shouldn't have left residing in you any intolerance. Or any self-consciousness either.

I don't think I'm especially unkind, but like so many of us, I know I possess a certain smug superiority. If we were driving along, I was capable of saying, "Will you look at that fat lady with the pink curlers and halter?"

And Alex would say, "Don't be mean, Daddy."

And I would say, "Oh, come on, Alex. I'm not being mean. She can't hear me."

And Alex replied—she really did—this way: "It is *too* mean, even if she can't hear you."

And, of course, that is altogether true. No matter what, Alex would never countenance any cruelty; she would never abide mockery in people, no matter how slight. Alex would not even permit us in the family to make a passing criticism about the way people *on television* wore their hair. So, after a while, we cut it out, and I'm sure we became better for it.

When Alex died, the sixth grade at her school, Greens Farms Elementary, wrote an especially nice letter telling us how much they admired Alex. We got a great deal of mail when Alex died, but most people—most grownups—went off in the wrong direction. It's a natural mistake, I guess; there is no primer to tell you what to write bereaved parents. Most people would go on at length about how difficult this must be for us, and what wonderful parents we had been—which is, in fact, about the last thing we wanted to hear, because it only made us feel more guilty. Let me tell you something: If a child dies and you console the parents, tell them about their child, don't write them about themselves.

The sixth grade did it right. They wrote about Alex, about how everybody at the school was aware of her, how she stood out for her pain and her courage. I know that none of us ever gets very comfortable about being different, and it is even more difficult for kids, because when you are young you are sure that you are the only different one in the whole class—the whole world. I wrote that class back: "The way you can best remember Alex is this: that everybody has something wrong with them, but that doesn't make them different. That makes us all the same, because we all share something wrong. So don't treat people different, because they aren't. But do treat them with care, because that is what we all need. That is the way Alex lived, and that is the way she wanted to be treated."

When Alex died we included in all the notices a request that contributions be sent to a special memorial account for her at the Cystic Fibrosis Foundation, the Alex Fund, we called it. It's unfortunate, but the only proper remembrances seem to be money or flowers. People were generous, but I wish Carol and I could have added, "In lieu of flowers, everybody who wants to honor the memory of Alexandra Deford should treat a person who is different with care and kindness."

CHAPTER 9

Instinctively, Alex began to understand how different she was before she began to look different. At ages four and five, between 1975 and 1976, when she was going to nursery school and kindergarten, she was still a little chubby. I once actually noted in her diary that she had lost some weight and looked a bit prettier for it. How innocent I was; in another couple of years I would have killed lions and tigers with my bare hands if that meant we could get a half-pound back on her. But at that time medicines and the treatments kept her on an even keel. Her clubbed fingers were not yet apparent to those who didn't know of her illness. Rarely did she cough between therapy sessions, when we forced up the mucus. Reluctantly, she put on pants in the winter and rarely missed a day of school.

But she knew. Alex knew something was up with her. She did not see herself as "special," either. We too often disguise the truth by employing that word to gloss over harsher truths—especially where children are involved. That is wrong. We are all made different. We make ourselves special. Alex was born different, but only as she grew did she become special, on her own hook. If you start off saying a child is special because she suffers from a handicap, that is a disservice, because you are robbing her of what she might become on her own.

59

Alex's nursery school class. At age four here, Alex, third from the left in the front row, is at her healthiest. You can see, she's almost chubby.

No doubt Alex was able to take cues from Carol and me. Given her young age, we never broached the seriousness of her disease with Alex, but I'm sure we inadvertently gave hints. By then I was exploring the subject, preparing myself, using the right people to help me, not unlike the way Alex used her dolls. I kidded myself a lot, too, reaching a little further into that abyss each time, but never truly admitting what I was up to. On the more obvious level, I became a little more curious with Tom Dolan and the other specialists I met. More subtly, I closely observed other cystic fibrosis parents—for example, those I encountered at trustee meetings.

We parents followed something of a conversational code there. Those trustees who had already lost their sick children could safely ask one another, "How's the family?" "How's everything at home?"—more or less like the lucky ones who had no CF kids. But for those of us with sick children, there was a dilemma. We did not want to charge in with "How're the kids?" because the answer might well be that a child was very sick and dying. I learned, from the way some scarred old hands approached the subject with me, to offer openings that were not leading. For example, "How old are your kids now?" or, "What grade are your children in this year?" Parents could then answer only the literal question, or, if they wanted, expand their reply and tell how their CF kids were doing.

I studied most closely the parents who had already lost children, examining them with morbid fascination. *How do they do it?* I asked myself. *How are they able to go on?* Even: Why *do they go on?* I wasn't sure I could. I wasn't sure I would want to if my child died. That attitude was a form of protection, too. Once you stopped thinking that way, once you decided that, yes, you could manage, then you were admitting a hard truth. So long as I thought that I could not cope, that I could not survive if Alex died, I could protect myself from admitting that Alex conceivably might die. Once I began to acknowledge that maybe I really could go on, as so many of my fellow trustees had, then I was likewise admitting to myself that Alex really could die.

Together, Carol and I protected ourselves—almost instinctively, I believe. We are, both of us, fairly candid people, but I search my memory now, and not once during those years without crisis do I ever recall the two of us sitting down and seriously discussing the worst possibilities ahead—that Alex would grow sicker and die. I knew Carol knew that; Carol knew I knew. To speculate would only have been masochistic. Likewise, Carol never once took it out on me

61

that I could often avoid the task of therapy—and the dreadful responsibility—whenever I traveled. Nor did I—much as she deserved it—make a big deal out of thanking Carol for the greater burden she had to carry most days. No, as it would have been pointless to dwell on death, it would have been ignoble to complain about the disease—because, really, that would have been complaining about Alex.

There were sad, telling episodes involving only myself and Alex that Carol never was aware of until she read the first draft of this book. And, likewise, Carol experienced moments of anguish and despair with Alex that I never knew of until now, when she recounted them to me for this book. One of the dearest—and most natural—things about child raising is when one parent can tell the other what little thing the child did each day. But somehow we sensed when it was best to deny each other that with Alex.

Somehow we understood that all sharing might not be good. After all, Alex was dying because of genes we shared. Carol and I sensed that talking about many things could strain the fragile links, already pulled so taut, as they are in every cystic fibrosis family. The trick, I suppose, was to avoid the truth just enough, and to escape just enough, but always to know that the avoidance and the escape were but temporary illusions to assure that Alex be permanent—permanent whether she was alive or dead.

That summer, when Alex was going on five, I wrote an article about cystic fibrosis for *Seventeen* magazine. The piece was about a teenaged patient named Lisa Boyle, and it told how she coped with the disease. I wanted to do what I could to tell people about CF, to publicize the disease, to display the bravery of the kids who suffered with it. But I always knew deep inside that I possessed an ulterior motive as well. By being with an older patient I could try and look into the future and obtain a glimpse of what Alex might be like growing up—and also, what I might be like then, too. My sincerity was tinged with some self-interest.

It is mocking to say, perhaps, but as these things go, Lisa was a relatively mild case. She was in her final year of high school, and she was going to make it to the other side of eighteen, the median age for survival; at least she lived long enough to make college. Lisa had two siblings, both sisters, both with CF. Her older sister had died many years ago as a child. A younger sister, Heather, was much worse off than Lisa. In fact, Heather was to die a few months later, before the article was published. The severity of her situation was painfully apparent that day I met all the Boyles.

The parents were wonderful people, and, at some point, alone with the father, I asked, "How do you do it?" I think he understood that I was not asking that question as part of the interview. I was really saying, "How will *I* do it? *Can* I do it?"

Much later, quite out of the blue, sometime after Heather had died, Jim Boyle wrote me a long letter, describing how Lisa was at college on the night Heather died at home. Lisa would die herself in a couple more years. She was a very bright girl who understood the odds. That night at college, when her parents told her that Heather could not even leave her oxygen long enough to come to the phone, Lisa understood. She went back to her dormitory room, found a prayer she liked, and copied it onto the picture of a Thanksgiving turkey that Heather had made for her. That was the last thing Heather had done for her sister. Then Lisa went to sleep, knowing that when she awoke her sister would be gone, as her older sister before her, as she herself soon enough.

"You asked how did we 'do it'?" Jim Boyle wrote me. "We reinforce each other in the struggle with cystic fibrosis. The memory of how Lisa handled her grief in this instance will always have special meaning to us. Most adults are wise enough to know that they learn something with each new experience from each passerby in their life. But to learn from a child, from your own child, is a beautiful thing. You will see."

And so we did.

CHAPTER 10

By 1975, a year after the pseudomonas was first diagnosed, I was well past the point of merely dealing with the possibility of Alex's death. I was carefully preparing myself for that. Shortly after her fourth birthday, I wrote this in the diary I kept for both children:

"Anyway, Alex may die before too long. This is so. I cannot bring myself to talk to Carol about this, though. It will only frighten us both more if we make the topic an official agenda item. But I must be very organized, for Alex, for us all. We must give her everything in life we can, and yet we must never make the giving more ostentatious than the life itself. Don't turn her life into a shopping list! And if she dies, if she must die, please, never waver with doubts about Heaven. She must always have a solid belief in the beyond. Already she talks about it so. She wants me to support her faith in that, as sure as Chris would like me to guarantee him that his Yankees will definitely, absolutely be in the World Series."

Still, we tried to give Alex as much as we could within the context of our existence. For instance, one time I took the whole family with me to Los Angeles when I went out on an assignment for *Sports Illustrated*. It was the depth of winter, and TWA had one of those deals going where they practically paid you to bring your family. Still, I probably wouldn't have lugged us all out there if it hadn't been for Alex. It was, no doubt, going to be her best chance to see California.

We had a fine time, too. My youngest brother Gill lives in Los Angeles, where he is a lawyer, so we had a home base there. Gill even got Alex invited to a neighborhood children's party, and as soon as her initial shyness departed she had such a dandy time that the rest of us just left her there. Gill took Chris to a baseball clinic the Dodgers were putting on, and Carol and I took a drive to see some sights.

In the next few years, as the CF worsened, Alex grew self-conscious about her appearance when she met new kids, but at this point she was quickly at ease with strange children. I suspect that had a lot to do with the fact that the visits to the clinic and hospital forced her to deal with strangers—children and grown-ups—regularly. Besides, she just plain liked people. By the time we came to pick Alex up from the party, she said she had so many new friends that she thought maybe we ought to move to California; or, at least, she could commute out there to parties. "I could stay with Gill," she said. "He doesn't have any little children, so I think he'd like it. And maybe you could pay him some money, too."

Even better than the party, though, was our motel, a Holiday Inn. Wherever you are in the world now, kids love the motels they stay in more than the Official Attractions they have come to see. Alex and Chris certainly did.

We had a terrific time. But Carol and I were determined that everybody—read Alex—would see the Pacific Ocean. Now, for a six-year-old—for most people of any age—an ocean is an ocean is an ocean; but we were hell-bent on Alex seeing the Pacific Ocean in her lifetime. Isn't it funny the things you think must be important? So, even though it was late in the day and all of us were tired and all everybody really wanted was to get a hamburger and go to a movie, Carol and I were resolved to fight our way to Santa Monica to view the Pacific Ocean—and to damn well appreciate it.

I drove that Hertz car like a bat out of hell, weaving in and out of traffic, down Wilshire, bound for Santa Monica. And, wouldn't you know it, a million-to-one chance, the car radio announced that atmospheric conditions at the moment would give L.A. its finest Pacific sunset in many years. I went heavier on the accelerator and the imagery. Not only were we going to see the sunset over the Pacific, we were going to see a better sunset than even Hollywood could make.

Terrific. The only thing was that Alex didn't care at all and neither did Chris. At that moment in time two things they had absolutely no interest in whatsoever were the Pacific Ocean and any sunset. As a matter of fact, even as we neared Santa Monica, even as I came on like Balboa about the glories we were about to see, Chris and Alex started screaming at us and squabbling with each other. Just west of the San Diego Freeway they all but came to blows.

"I want a Coke."

"Why are we going out here?"

"I thought you said we could see a movie."

"Get over to your side."

"I'm not even going to look at the stupid ocean."

And so forth.

It was all I could do, in my utter conviction of knowing what was best for her, not to turn around and scream, "Damnit, Alex, you are dying, and so I'm going to show you the Pacific Ocean!"

We did finally reach the Ocean Highway at almost the exact moment that winter's early night curtain fell. If you strained you could see the last visible rays of the sun forming a sliver of light on the water. And, not leaving bad enough alone, I then turned the car north, and drove up to Malibu, where, in the pitch dark, Alex could get an even better view of an ocean she could not see.

Finally, duty done, we had a nice dinner and saw a movie that Alex enjoyed as much as anything on the whole trip, though she could have seen the same film back home in Westport. Still, if you woke me up in the middle of the night and asked me to name the things Alex did in her life, I would probably mention that she saw a sunset over the Pacific Ocean at the very top of the list.

But then, maybe I—we all—survived because however impossible, however appalling, it was that our child was dying, I could sometimes still see the whimsy that forever cloaks the pain and the hopelessness of life.

Alex was never all sadness. What made her illness especially difficult was that she was such a happy child, that she produced so much joy for those around her. And, sick as she was, she had a wonderful capacity to rise to the special treat. Best of all were the few Broadway shows she saw—*Annie* was her favorite. She also went to the Rockettes and an Orioles-Yankees game, to the top of the Empire State Building, and out to the Statue of Liberty. She saw the dinosaurs at the Museum of Natural History, the Hayden Planetarium, and the *Nutcracker* ballet at Christmastime. Every year, when my friend Richard Dwyer, the star of the Ice Follies, would come into New Haven, he would get us front-row seats and then give us a backstage tour. Alex saw the Tall Ships enter New York harbor on July 4, 1976, and she met Gov. Ella Grasso and Jimmy Connors when she was the poster child for the Connecticut Cystic Fibrosis Foundation chapter. She and Governor Grasso gave out the awards at the Aetna World Cup, a tennis tournament that helped benefit the foundation. It was an election year, and Governor Grasso stayed very close to Alex. Alex liked Governor Grasso, too, because we told her that she was the first woman in the United States ever to be elected governor on her own. Governor Grasso wore a bright cherry-red pants suit. Alex was in pigtails with a pink dress—pink was, usually, her favorite color—and long white socks and patent leather shoes. I have all that on home movies. And Alex was dead in two years and Governor Grasso in three.

Alex with Ella Grasso, America's first elected female governor, in March 1978 at the Aetna World Cup, a tennis tournament. Alex was the poster girl for CF, which was the beneficiary of the tournament. Governor Grasso herself died a few years later, of cancer.

Alex visited the aquarium at Old Mystic, Connecticut (featuring Alex the Whale; but he's a boy Alex), and she went to Williamsburg, where, best of all she enjoyed learning about how eighteenth-century ladies used their fans to send amorous messages to their beaus. She saw the Old Man of the Mountain up in New Hampshire and she saw Miss America crowned at Convention Hall in Atlantic City one of the years I was a judge. She went to Florida and saw alligator farms, a snake farm, the Monkey Jungle, the Waltzing Waters, and Cypress Gardens. Plus Disney World and some neat motels. She saw the sights in Washington, D.C., and once she even got out of the country. That was in March 1979 when some friends of ours, Ann and Harvey Clapp, invited us to stay with them in St. Croix.

So Alex did see and do a lot for a little girl who barely lived eight years.

Inevitably, though, there were many things we never did manage to do. Like visiting where Ruffian was buried. Like a circus. Like Hawaii. That was the ultimate. Alex always dreamed of Hawaii. It was far enough away and different enough to be exotic, but it was American, televised all the time. Hawaii is a most practical fantasy. Besides, above all else in the world, Alex loved dancing, and so hula was right up her alley. When she was five years old and I traveled there, I brought her back leis and a hula skirt, and she loved to dress up in them. Alex dreamed of Hawaii. In her happiest times alone, playing with her dolls, the dolls were taking trips to Hawaii. Or they had just arrived back, all suntanned. Certainly she never permitted any dolls to die in Hawaii. Alex would say that when she was grown up and didn't have to do therapy anymore, "When they have a cure for my disease, when I'm free, I think maybe I'll live in Hawaii." She had that uppermost in her mind.

Of course, Hawaii was a long way and a lot of money from Connecticut, and so I never led her down the garden path when it came to Hawaii. In fact, what I started to promise Alex was that when they did find a cure for cystic fibrosis, I would take the whole family on the next plane to Honolulu, and we would stand on the beach at Waikiki and toast in champagne.

"You mean I could have champagne even though I'm not a lady?" she said.

"Alex, the day they find the cure, you can drink champagne or anything you want anywhere you want."

And Alex would even tell people that, that she had an extra lot to look forward to, because when they found the cure for her disease, she wasn't just going to stop doing therapy and stop taking medicines and all that, she was going to Hawaii, too.

Then when the Clapps invited us to St. Croix we had a terrific time, and Carol and I could point out to Alex that St. Croix was a tropical island just like Hawaii. So, when we came back home I started thinking, *Alex loved that so much and she wants to go to Hawaii so much, next year we will all go to Hawaii, and never mind how much it costs.*

Well, thank God, I never came right out and told Alex that. In May, only a few weeks after we got back from St. Croix, she had to go back into the hospital, and that time it was more serious than ever before. She deteriorated quickly after that, and there never was another spring or another chance to go to Hawaii.

Well, at least not while Alex was alive. But just before the next Christmas, 1980, Carol and Chris and I did go to Hawaii. And we went largely because of Alex, which made it especially hard for us. I cried, not only because Alex wasn't in Hawaii, which was the one place on the face of the earth where she always wanted to go, but because the rest of us were there—and we were there for the very reason that she had died.

I kept telling myself not to feel guilty. There was nothing more I could do for Alex. I had given her all the love I

71

could, everything I was capable of. But still, that was only a bunch of rational stuff. She had wanted so much to do that one thing, to go to Hawaii, and I put it off and put it off, and soon enough there was no way we could get there together.

And what worries me is that Heaven might end up to be the same elusive sort of thing.

CHAPTER 11

School buses are always the most painful of re-
minders. At once they remind me of Alex then and make me
consider where she would be now.

When an adult dies, even when one dies fairly young,
I think we accept that person forever as an ageless adult. If
John dies when he is twenty-five, I don't think people look at
his best buddies years later and conjure up John, too, as bald-
ing and overweight and hopelessly middle-aged. With children it's different. Alex was eight when she died, and while I
cannot, in my wildest dreams, conceive of her as a grown
woman, the opposite does apply.

I see her friends getting older, I see her with them,
and at the same time I am crying out that they must stop.
Please, please! Each time I see Wendy or Aimee or any of them
appearing older it hurts me more, for they are the most direct
links I have with Alex, they are the contemporary connection.
Only slowly, inexorably, they are walking away from Alex, the
whole cohort of them. Alex is forever eight, and now they are
eleven, then twelve, soon thirteen, and then sweet sixteen and
twenty-one, and each day they grow older, Alex turns more
into memories.

I can hardly remember myself at eight; how are we expected to remember anybody else at eight years old? "My

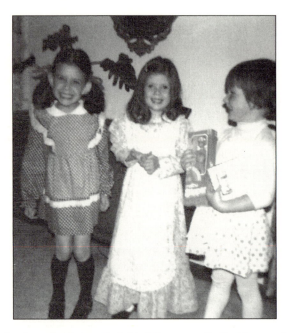

Alex at what is probably her sixth birthday party, flanked by good friends
Aimee on the left and Wendy on the right.

God," Carol said the other day, apologizing in some way,
"I'm having trouble remembering how she talked. I don't
really remember how she sounded anymore."

So, the school buses are the worst. They rattle down
the street, beyond the lawn in front of my office window.
They never stop near our house. The neighborhood kids all
gather down at the corner of Devon Road, out of my sight.
The last couple years, when Alex was weaker, the bus drivers,
without being asked, started letting her off right in front of
our house. She would struggle down the steps—that last step
off any school bus is a monster for any kid—catch her breath,
and then amble up the driveway to the house, reviewing what
she was going to tell Carol or me about her adventures at

school that day. Sometimes, in good weather, I would wait outside behind an azalea bush, and jump out at her. If the kids on the bus could see this buffoonery—from a certified father!—it would absolutely mortify Alex. "Oh, Daddy, please don't embarrass me like that," she would say.

Alex's very first bus ever came at 8:15 A.M., Tuesday, the seventh of September 1976. A whole throng of neighborhood children were there, Chris, the veteran, included, and rookies Aimee and Wendy, too, and Carol was there to send Alex off, but still she clambered up the steps with a great deal of trepidation. However, the instant the cord was cut, she pranced to her seat and was fine. This was a common brand of behavior for Alex, even on occasions when she was somewhat experienced in the adventure. "Alex, why do you act like this?"

"Oh, Daddy, that's what being shy is."

Miss Linder was Alex's kindergarten teacher at Greens Farms Elementary. In her first report she found Alex "cooperative, conscientious, and well-mannered." There was some good news and some bad news. "Occasionally, she holds her flashcards in an upside down or backwards position. . . . Alex also has been working with Mrs. Ikard in an adaptive physical education program. Mrs. Ikard reports that Alex tries very hard and is showing progress."

This latter was a nice teacherese way of saying that Alex was hopelessly uncoordinated. It took her forever to learn to put on her underpants or to hold a pencil. When she first got on a tricycle, she promptly fell off and wouldn't dare remount for months. Alex was, quite simply, a klutz. That Chris happens to be well coordinated made it ironic, and it would have been otherwise inconsequential, except for one thing.

Cystic fibrosis is one of the rare diseases from which females suffer worse than males. Beginning about the age of seven or eight, girls die at a faster rate. Nobody can explain

75

this disparity, but most doctors suspect that whatever physio-logical factors may be at play, cultural conditioning is even more important. Little boys—even little boys with CF—tend to go out and play ball games, roughhouse, run around, and build up their lungs in those ways. Little girls—probably es-pecially little girls with CF—dress up, play with dolls, and lead a more sedentary existence. Their lungs aren't tested.

It doesn't matter all that much. Not in the long run. It wouldn't have saved Alex if she had swum the English Channel. Still, we kept wishing that she would want to be more athletic. Who knows? It might have been just enough to have kept her alive until the time when they would knock out pseudomonas, and then . . .

Anyway, Carol did get Alex going to a dance class. It was run by a lovely young woman named Marlayne Schaeffer, who later was to help tutor Alex in her regular schoolwork. The dance class—styled authoritatively as *ballet* by Alex—was her delight, and, surely, the first time in her life that she really enjoyed something physical. She was relatively proficient at it, too; she had great confidence in her body when she was danc-ing, and that had an impact on all the rest of her. "I never saw a child come out of herself so quickly as Alex did," Marlayne told Carol. "At first she was a little inhibited, but then she would get this lovely look on her face just watching the others dance."

Slowly, Alex became more venturesome. For once in her life she found out that she could make her body obey, make it work, and that enthralled her. It proved that she wasn't as un-coordinated as she and the rest of us all thought. I came to believe, in fact, that if she had put an equivalent effort into bike riding or swimming or throwing a ball, she could have become proficient at those, too. But dance was the only phys-ical activity she ever threw herself into, and I'm sure now it was that same selective instinct of hers. Alex understood that time was short for her, and that she had to choose.

In Alex's last months, when she began to miss so much school, Marlayne, who had been an elementary teacher, would come over and tutor Alex at home in her regular classroom subjects. She was way behind in arithmetic by then, but she couldn't be bothered with struggling to make it up. "Math was just not important to her by then," Marlayne says. It was like riding a bicycle.

So she and Marlayne would mostly read and write, Alex testing her imagination and her creativity. They would go outside and pick flowers, and then Alex would make up stories about them. She was supposed to work on her writing, but sometimes, weak and impatient, she would make up the story faster than she could write it down, so she would ask Marlayne to write it for her. This one, for example, she dictated in October 1979, three months before she died.

The Dancers' Surprise!
Once upon a time there was a little dance group, and they were doing a dance, but they didn't have money to buy costumes. So, they were all sitting in the garden. The warm sunshine put them in a trance, and, all of a sudden something very strange happened.
All the geraniums in the garden magically turned into tutus!
Well, you can imagine the surprise when the dancers woke up!
They jumped up and put on the tutus and danced a dance they called the geranium waltz!
The End

While she was still healthy enough, dance gave Alex her favorite creative outlet. She enjoyed it most, too, when

Marlayne introduced props into the activity—scarves to whirl about, bright objects to brandish. Then Alex could even prevail as a performer over the girls who could dance physically better than she.

When Alex did her creating by herself, away from classrooms and dance studios and other people, she called it *imagining*. That was her word; her best word, I think. Alex was a big fan of Beverly Sills, and she even came to feel some identification with her, because Carol told Alex about how Beverly Sills had a daughter who was deaf, who had never been able to hear her own mother's beautiful voice. And one evening, when Carol visited Alex in the hospital, there she was alone in her room, watching Beverly Sills in *La Traviata* on television.

"But Alex," Carol said, "don't you have trouble understanding what's going on, since you don't know what any of the words mean?"

"Oh, no, Mother. It's better this way, because then I can make it all up. I'm just having a good time imagining."

Like some witch doctor who wears a mask to help conjure up friendly spirits, Alex liked to assist the pure imaginating by wearing special costumes. Almost all little girls like to dress up, I know, but Alex made a fetish of it. Her everyday costume included large earrings, many bracelets, a (perennial) scarf in her hair, plus a long gown of some sort, simulated or real.

Sometimes Alex would just make up stuff out of the blue, as with the flowers *cum* tutus. Other times, like most artists, she would borrow from the world around her, as when she gave therapy to her dolls. One time, after she had witnessed a christening at church, I came into her room to find her, fully bedecked as usual in earrings and scarves, but portraying a minister. She had constructed an altar and had a doll there. "What are you doing, Alex?"

"Can't you see, Daddy? I'm bap-a-tizing."

Another favorite activity was "doing commercials," with the bathroom mirror serving as TV screen. She could ad lib, too. Here's what Jake Weinstock wrote in class shortly after Alex died:

> Things I Remeber With Alex
> At a cookout last year I was playing pingpong with Nicky and Alex was watching and I made a bad serve and the ball hit Alex and she fell on the floor like she was knocked out.

Not bad. Whenever Alex was asked to write down the things that she would like to be when she grew up, she would always put "Dancer" first and "Actress" second. I think she fancied herself as a dancer first because then she could dream that if ever she did grow up, she would be able to whirl about endlessly and gracefully, never having to stop and pause for breath, to excuse herself and sit down to catch up.

When she was in Marlayne's dance class and she had to stop for a while, Alex would not, even then, moan or whine. She would not upset the ballet that way. It was not the dance's fault that she could not go on; it was her disease's fault, and she understood that. So she would just sit down until she could catch her breath, all the while smiling and laughing at all the lucky little girls still out there dancing. And she would imaginate, too.

A few months after Alex died, Marlayne and the other dancers in her local troupe, which was known as Kinetikos, put on a show at the YMCA, where dance classes were held in Westport. Afterward, all of them—Marlayne and Cindy Bernier, Lindy Gibb and Joan Chess—dedicated something to Alex. It was their own perfect idea: a huge old trunk, as much like a pirate's treasure chest as could be found. And inside it were all sorts of old clothes and costumes that kids could put

This is a view of Greens Farms School a day or two after Alex died—with the flag flying at half-mast in her memory.

on whenever they felt like it. A portrait of Alex hung over the chest, watching. And it was called "The Imaginating Trunk."

Alex's memorial at Greens Farms School is a little section of the common room, which has been named "Alex's Corner." Bright rainbow letters, posted high, label it as such. There is a desk there, with Alex's smiling picture on it, some books and games and puzzles, and a few beanbag chairs of green and yellow, so that any child has a place to go and relax and find a moment's peace.

As Alex got sicker and weaker, she couldn't run around at recess. And that upset her. Recess. Remember when you were a child? It's universal and timeless: *What's your favorite subject?*

Recess.

So that separated her more than ever. She would hang back, watching all the other kids scampering around, scrambling over the jungle gyms. The teachers would come over and talk to Alex, try and divert her, but they never had much success. Recess was the one time, it seemed, when even Alex would feel sorry for herself.

And so that is why the school decided to construct Alex's Corner, because whenever there is another sick child like Alex, or if only for a day or two some little girl or boy can't go out for recess, at least they'll have a place where they can go and find some peace and maybe even imaginate if they want to.

CHAPTER 12

It was barely a month after Alex first climbed onto her school bus that she had to leave school and go back into the hospital, for the first time since the crisis in her infancy. There was no denying that the decline had set in. I certainly didn't know that there were barely three years left in her life, but I understood enough of the situation to write: "How cruel is this? One day you send your baby off to kindergarten, to start her school, and the next day you take her to the hospital to begin to die."

The timetable was to be a simple one, too. At first, Alex would go in every six months for ten-day treatments. There was never any urgency then: When would it be convenient for Alex to go in sometime soon? But before long those periods between visits began to shorten, and eventually the time in the hospital began to lengthen, too. In the end, all we prayed was that she might be able to come home and die. That's the way it went. That is what a *progressive* disease is. It's an odd use of the word, isn't it?

If there was a saving grace in those early, ten-day hospital sojourns, it was that they were as smooth as a child could expect. Essentially, all the doctors did was to give Alex antibiotics intravenously instead of orally, as she normally took them at home. This constant, concentrated dosage fought the pseudomonas in her lungs more effectively, and, we hoped, made her stronger. Weighing her was the climax of every day. "Alex gained a half pound!" Carol would cry out to me, as if we had just won the lottery.

But once the IV was in place, lodged in one of the veins on the back of her hand—left first, then right—Alex's existence in the hospital was quite routine. Yale–New Haven is a teaching hospital, so invariably interns came by to study her, and there would be periodic X rays and visits by Tom Dolan and his associates in the CF clinic, but these things were all pretty cursory. Most of the time Alex could watch television, read, work at some activity in her room, or get involved in the little hospital school or with the crafts program.

On that first visit, in October 1976, Carol slept over for the first couple of nights on a cot next to Alex's bed. This was not an uncommon procedure for kids new to the hospital, but, obviously, it wasn't something Carol could do every night. We tried to be tough about sleeping over with her, and, in fact, we could pretty much measure Alex's mood by whether or not she dwelled on the subject. The sadder and more unpleasant things were, the more she would beg Carol to stay the night. I had lied at first and told her they did not allow daddies to sleep over, and Alex bought that for a while, but eventually she started pleading with me, too.

Carol and I never did know what was right. Can you imagine how you would feel, leaving your sick kid behind in a hospital, while she begs you to stay? But we knew that Alex would have to spend many days and many nights in a hospital for the rest of her life, and I don't believe that she would have adjusted so well to that if she knew that Mommy or Daddy was going to be there every night. In a way, she had to establish her own independent existence in that hospital ward.

All hospitals have strict rules about healthy children visiting their siblings or friends, but we were allowed to bring Chris to see Alex on Sundays, and that was always the high

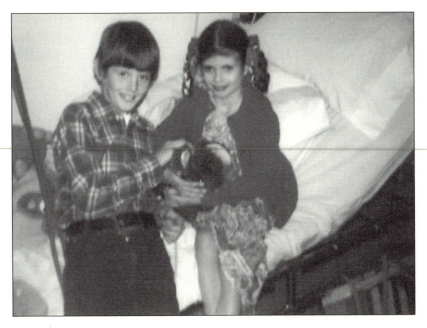

"Chrish" was finally allowed to visit Alex in the hospital just a few weeks before she died.

point of her stays. "Oh, Chrish!" she would call out, and her face would light up and her cheeks bloom. Usually, she would want to introduce him—show him off—to some new friend she had made. She was so proud of him. Never once in Alex's life, no matter how angry or frustrated she might get, did she wish cystic fibrosis on her brother or cry out that it was unfair that she had it and he didn't.

Nobody really knows how much psychological effect this disease has on healthy siblings. Obviously, as they gain maturity, most of them will feel some guilt that the angel of death somehow passed by their bedroom door, even as it struck the one just down the hall. Cystic fibrosis scars everyone in a family, one way or another. There were also times when Chris whined that Alex got away with murder and drew

85

more of our love and attention because she was sick—a few times, even, when he roughed her up a little in his anger—but probably he was right, and surely every brother acts like that occasionally with a kid sister.

Those were the exceptions, though. Chris was loving and protective with Alex even when he was only five or six, and he would get up weekend mornings when we were trying to sleep late to go downstairs and fix breakfast for himself and his little sister. Just cereal and juice at first, then he added ready-mix pancakes to his culinary repertoire. And no matter what we threatened him with—no TV, no baseball—most every night he would leave his room and go sleep in the same bed with Alex. How could you stay mad at him for that? There in the morning they would be, Chris all curled up under the covers, Alex sprawled outside them. For some reason, she almost always kicked off the covers on her side.

Chris never let himself admit how sick his sister was. I imagined that he knew much more than he let on, but I realized later that he didn't know as much as I assumed. I had made the mistake of thinking that Chris could be as mature and practical about Alex's illness as she was. It was always easy to forget how grown-up Alex was about herself.

And yet it was disconcerting. Whereas Alex could deal with the fact that she had an incurable disease, she would absolutely dissolve at the prospect of having another IV stuck in her—especially since she knew she was so skinny that there was so little of her to work with, that the doctors would probably have to try over and over again. Sticking her, jabbing her, hurting her. It was never really the going into the hospital that upset Alex. No, it was going into the hospital and getting a needle. Barbara Arends, Alex's favorite nurse, told me, "No matter how many times Alex came in, and no matter how good a patient she was, she was never really herself until the IV was in, and *she* was sure it was in good. The doctor might tell her it was fine, but she wouldn't necessarily believe him, because she knew better about needles than they did."

Even I sometimes forgot that Alex was only a little girl. I would be surprised every time when grown-ups would visit Alex in the hospital and how they would be surprised by the candor of her conversations with the doctors who dropped by. And the trouble is, the better a patient you are, the more people start thinking of you as a patient first and whatever else you are—little girl, grown man, whatever—next.

"Please stay over tonight, Daddy."

"Oh, come on, Alex, you know I can't."

"Oh, please, Daddy. I'll go right to bed, and you can stay up late and read your book. Please."

"Alex, you know I can't stay. Now be a good girl."

Pause. "Well, when you go home, will you ask Mother if she can stay with me tomorrow night?"

And I would go home from that awful place, hating myself, go home to my wife and son, hating them, too. I suppose, hating us all that we could be at home, together, healthy, while Alex stayed in the hospital, alone, sick. "Well," Carol would say, "at least we don't have to wake up extra early tomorrow and do therapy." And we would nod lamely at each other, all the more guilty that we did *not* have to do therapy. And it's funny, too, but the truth is that a lapse in a routine—any routine, even one you hate—makes you all the more aware of what is missing.

So we would have our breakfast, the three of us, and Alex's school bus would come by. At first, when she went into the hospital, the bus would sort of pause outside our house— waiting for a moment, almost like some great horse nodding in anticipation—as if Alex must just be late, and would be rushing out the door in another moment. But then, as the days went by, the bus wouldn't stop and wait at all. It would just roar by, never even slowing down.

87

For Alex, I think, the worst part of the hospital was simply that she had to spend time there—away. It was one final, obvious certification that she was different. If it had only been the pain—even the IV needles—she could have handled that. But for her the great fear was wondering how others would react to her.

This happened when Alex was six and a half, when I told her some friends of ours were coming out from New York to have dinner.

"Can I dress up in my favorites?"

"Of course you can. We want you to look great."

"Neat-ooo!" She started to skip away, happily. But then she stopped. "Maybe I better stay in my room."

"Why?"

"Well, do they know about my disease, Daddy?"

"Sure they do."

"Okay, then they won't laugh at me when I cough, will they?"

Nonetheless, from all that I know, there was only one occasion in which Alex was treated cruelly, singled out as some freak. I checked this out with Christian regularly, too, and I asked Wendy and Aimee about it after Alex died; they all assured me that nobody ever teased Alex for her differences, that if anybody had tried, the other kids wouldn't have tolerated it.

But there was this one time. As Alex got sicker and her clubbed fingers grew paler and more bulbous from the lack of oxygen, she became more self-conscious about them, sure everybody was staring. And, of course, she was probably right. Clubbed fingers really are different, not like coughing or being skinny.

One day when a new family moved into our neighborhood some of the veteran kids ran over to fill the newcomers in on the territory. By the time Alex met the new kids, they had heard all about her, the little girl down on the

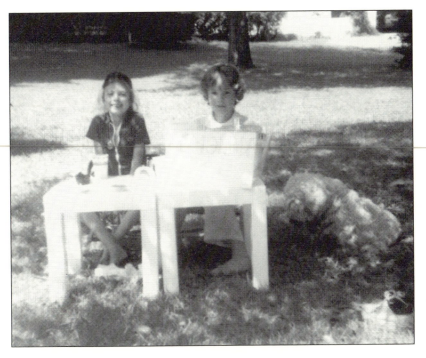

Alex and Wendy selling lemonade, with Chaucer's help.

corner who had this cystic fibrosis disease. What's that? Well, she coughs, but don't worry, she doesn't give you germs, but she has to take all these medicines all the time, and she's always going to the hospital, and she's skinny and you should see these weirdo funny fingers she has.

Then, when Alex dropped over, probably not looking nearly as peculiar as the new kids figured a "disease person" would look, one of them said, "Let me see your funny fingers."

And Alex ran right home, crying. I was there. She fell into my arms. "They *told,* Daddy! They told the new kids about my fingers." And I let her cry all she wanted. She sobbed for a long time, too, and didn't want to go back outside. I tried to tell her something philosophical, but luckily I stopped in time, because I realized how empty that would sound. A child who is different, who has just been singled out and hurt for being different, is beyond fancy philosophy. Instead, we just hugged some more.

I don't remember Alex mentioning her fingers again, and, as far as I know, there never was another incident. But sometime after she died, her grown-up friend Cyd Slotoroff, who played the guitar and sang for the kids in the hospital, told me that once she and Alex had been talking about secrets. Alex said she had a secret. First she told Cyd about that episode with the new neighbors and about how she had been betrayed.

"Is that your secret?" Cyd asked.

"No, that's not my secret," Alex said. "Daddy knew about that."

"So what's your secret?"

Alex dropped her eyes. She looked at her fingers. Then she balled both her hands up into fists. "Sometimes I do this, Cyd. I do this, so I won't have to see my own fingers."

"Yes," Cyd said.

"That's my secret."

CHAPTER 13

Cystic fibrosis kills children, and painfully. How much worse could a thing be that kills children? But cystic fibrosis *is* worse. It can threaten the whole family in many ways, destroy the hearts and the faith of all its members. Whenever I was away from home, traveling on business, I felt as if some great burden had been lifted from me. And yet, I always felt guilty for leaving home—never mind that I had to, that it was my job, our livelihood. Whenever I returned, I could see the weariness in Carol, the deeper anguish in her eyes.

Directly because of this, the autumn Alex was four Carol returned to school at a local community college, where she studied to become a registered nurse. I certainly didn't tell her at the time, but I don't think she especially wanted to be a nurse. Instead, I think that field of study best let her justify her decision to go back to college. She knew she would have felt guilty if she had just taken a normal liberal arts curriculum—some mere scholastic excuse to escape the house and the growing pall of the disease. But any medical training she received was bound to come in handy with Alex. So, nursing.

Still, I knew; however much the schooling might help Carol treat Alex, that was secondary. She *needed* something that would require her to leave the house, force her to

91

concentrate on something—anything—other than cystic fibrosis. And sure enough, while the nursing program was a tiring regimen, it breathed new spirit into Carol.

Unfortunately, just as Carol started her second year, Alex had to go back into the hospital, so Carol had to withdraw from college. The disease had expanded once more, to fill an even larger place in Alex's life, in all our lives. For the first time, regular hospitalization was a fact, the conclusions unavoidable. Although we did not appreciate it at the time, that year was the worst experience Chris ever had in school. We probably failed him in many ways during that period. We'll never know how much damage the whole experience did to him.

By the next fall, 1977, Carol had grown even more desperate. Cystic fibrosis was encircling her. She told me that she had to go back to college, to something that took her mind and body alike away from the disease. "I can't just go get a job in a store, Frank," she said. "That wouldn't be enough to put CF out of my mind. You're lucky. When you write, you can concentrate, and—and—"

"I know."

"That's what I need. Something I really have to focus on, something really demanding. So I have to forget. At least some."

She found a special liberal education program at Sarah Lawrence College, and it seemed perfect. Intellectually, it was far more difficult than the nursing school, but it was nowhere near as unbending in its scheduling demands. If some crisis came up with Alex, Carol could adjust and still find a way eventually to catch up back at school. She was just thrilled when Sarah Lawrence accepted her.

Carol was still almost a full two years short of a bachelor's degree. She had given up education after junior college to go to New York, and she was living there, breaking in as a fashion model, when we met again, three years after that first, desultory encounter in college. Obviously, she had grown apace; she had her wits about her. She was no longer a mere college girl, but a grown woman of sagacity and judgment. In other words, she bought my act this time around.

Actually, though we were both living in New York when we met again, that Labor Day weekend of 1964, the encounter took place at a beach in Delaware. We took up back in Manhattan and were married the next summer. Carol kept on with her modeling. She was what is known as a "runway model," meaning she just did fashion shows. For some reason, she tensed up before a camera and didn't show herself to best advantage there. Linda Evans can sleep nights. Carol gave up modeling three years after we got married, when she became pregnant with Chris. Then Alex came. Carol always planned to go back to *some*thing when the two kids grew up, but she never seriously envisioned that she would escape back to college. In fact, Carol graduated from Sarah Lawrence, and with A's, too, but by then Alex was dead. Carol continued going on for her master's, in social work.

As draining as it was for Carol to be so responsible for Alex, she was fortunate in one way. As a writer, I have a more flexible schedule and I work at home a lot, so when I was not traveling, I was there to help with everyday responsibilities. But there is an awful, ironic hook that comes with a disease like cystic fibrosis. No matter how much I was around, Carol and I discovered that we could not depend upon one another.

Such a tragedy as ours does not bring a family together the way it's supposed to in the movies and the uplift books. The problem was that each of us needed to draw the same consolation from each other. Carol told me not long ago that support comes in many subtle forms, and that she always knew somehow I was there with her; but great as any love may be, it is never enough to turn the trick by itself. How, in desperation—guilty, angry, frustrated, scared—how could I turn for solace to my wife, the mother of my child, when she was

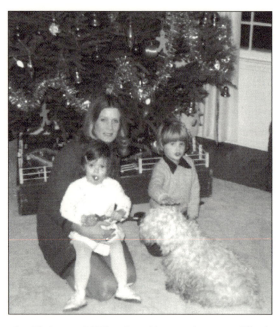

This had to be Christmas 1973, when Alex was just two. That's a young Chris petting Chaucer. Tragedy does bring a family together, but not always as it's portrayed in movies and books.

the mother of the child dying, and going through all the same as I, wanting the same thing I did? How do you give the very thing you need more of yourself? Believe me, I'm not just letting myself off easy when I say that it is much more complicated a matter than mere selfishness.

Whatever happened, I felt that I was failing Carol, that I was unable to help her and comfort her when she needed me most. But, in the same way, I resented that she could not help me when I wanted help, too—even though I understood why.

When our child was dying—when she was dying because of the genes we passed on to her—no matter how irrational it may have been to flagellate ourselves, there were times, in the mustiest corners of self-awareness, when we had to. Had to. I could not forgive Carol any more than I could forgive myself. After all, we quickly enough assume credit for the genes that make any of our children attractive and bright—*she takes after me.* It's only human nature, then, that we also accept the responsibility when we pass on genes of destruction. No, I did not really kill my child, and it profits nothing to dwell on that, but neither can I avoid the ultimate irony that simultaneously I created a life and a death, together.

I came to hate it—hate her, I suppose—when Carol would tell me how something else, something new, had gone wrong with Alex, how something worse had been discovered. *Don't tell me,* I was screaming inside. I don't want to be responsible. I don't want to be anybody's father. And Carol would get just as furious at me, because I would not respond as she wanted me to; I wouldn't evidence enough concern or distress.

But it was almost a studied pose I had chosen. I knew how bad the whole business was. I knew where Alex was heading. I knew how much hope it was emotionally safe for me to assume. So when Carol would tell me more bad news, what did it matter, really? If not today, then tomorrow. I felt that if I downplayed sad new developments, it would be better for us both than if I merely echoed Carol's despair. But why should I be surprised when she got mad at me for that? You see, there were also times when I was the one especially depressed about Alex, and if Carol did not seem to me properly sorrowful, I would loathe her for her callousness or envy her the ability to escape for the moment. There was no way to win. Grief was bad company, and optimism was no antidote.

No wonder, then, that so many cystic fibrosis families come apart at the seams. The process is often speeded up when the father, in extreme machismo, refuses to help with treatment, refuses even to acknowledge that his child is different, sick, weak, and dying with a disease he passed on. In a survey of CF families, the constant home treatment program was cited as the most difficult aspect of the disease. Second was the fact that the burden of care fell on one parent. Invariably, of course, that was the mother. And then, following in order, families mentioned the financial problems, the specter of death, the pressure from unfeeling relatives, the shame and disgrace of the disease's hereditary quality, and—full circle—the added fear of pregnancy, of giving birth to another dying child.

Ultimately, whether in my dealings with Carol, with Alex herself, with anyone involved with the disease—or with myself, for that matter—the major emotion pressing upon me was the feeling of inadequacy. Of course, I rationally understood that I could not cure my child, but day upon day, to work with her, to help her, to hold out hope for her, and yet still to see her deteriorate before my eyes—that was an experience that suggested the hopelessness of life as much as anything I can imagine. The most lost of lost causes is the one for which you must continue to apply effort even when you know it is pointless. And I could neither satisfactorily console my wife nor guide my healthy son through this awful thicket. And I could not explain how I felt, because of the shame, nor could I ever escape, because of the guilt. Even when I went to the hospital I felt bad, because there I would encounter all those wonderful volunteers who worked selflessly, not for obvious personal reasons, as I did.

So often I think I would have cracked, except for Alex herself and her example. People told me how terrific or brave or noble I was, and I hated them for that, even as I did appreciate their caring. But me? I am not dying. I am not sick. I am not in pain. It is my child to whom I bequeathed these things. I really don't think it's possible to be a good parent in such a situation. All you can hope to do is to manage, to survive. I'm a survivor; that's all. The only hero, ever, was Alex. And the older she got, the more her prospects dimmed, the finer and stronger a human being she became.

CHAPTER 14

Carol and I were fortunate in one regard, because my company, Time Inc., has a bountiful medical plan. Out of pocket, after being reimbursed by insurance, Alex's disease probably cost us about a thousand dollars a year, but nothing near what it could have, what it costs other CF families who are unable to obtain sufficient medical insurance. I am aware of young adults with the disease whose expenses may approach a thousand dollars *a day* when they must be hospitalized. But we were among the lucky families.

I would always get these little statements from Blue Cross a few weeks after Alex had been released from the hospital. They looked exactly like bills, and were obviously designed to make you think, at first unwitting glance, that they were indeed bills, even though it was stated somewhere on them, "This Is Not a Bill." They would read $9,741 or $12,639 or some such thing, and were intended to scare hell out of you before you realized they were not bills. Then you would be eternally grateful for Blue Cross and would accept rate hikes without so much as a whimper.

We were blessed with a lot of support in our extended families, too. There were times, when Alex was younger and healthier, when Carol and I could get away for long weekends because Carol's mother would come up and stay with Chris and Alex, managing the therapy herself. Sometimes we were even able to steal a few days' vacation by dropping the kids off with my parents in Baltimore. My mother learned how to do some of the therapy, and she also had a professional come in once a day. But as Alex got older and began to decline, that was no longer really feasible.

In the spring of 1977, Alex's kindergarten year, I was assigned a story in Japan, and it was such a rare opportunity that I wanted Carol to come along. I knew she desperately needed a respite from cystic fibrosis. But we had to find someone who could stay with the kids and care for Alex. Our good friends Tina and Jay Crawford volunteered to take on the assignment, and they were perfect for the task. Their little boy, Jonah, was in Alex's class, and he worshiped Chris as a hero. More important, Tina was a nurse and psychologist, and she already knew how to perform postural drainage. In the years left to Alex, Tina would become her adult nonfamily confidante around home, just as Cyd or Barbara and some of the other nurses fulfilled that role at the hospital. So, off we went to the Far East.

Alex could print capital letters by then. I have a sheet of paper from February of that year with the names of an interesting variety of foodstuffs carefully carved out, alphabetically, in red pencil—starting with apple and banana and continuing right on through upside-down cake and zwieback. But her mind was really starting to race, and Alex was often talking and "imaginating" much too fast for her careful letter making to keep up. Ironically—but perhaps not surprisingly— Alex's intellect grew stronger as she started going into the hospital on a regular basis. Part of that was surely because she was constantly around adults, but I also suspect that the hospital heightened her own sense of the time left to her. Mrs. Patricia Beasley, who was Alex's last teacher, in the third grade, told me after she died, "I could always detect a certain urgency with Alex. She was so anxious to try and catch up.

There was such an impatience to her, and it took me awhile to understand that mostly she was just frustrated that this disease interfered with the rest of her life."

Whatever the reason, Alex's spoken vocabulary, her whole comprehension, moved leaps and bounds beyond the primitive block letters she was carving out at school. I was fascinated one time when Alex started off on a careful explanation of the Save the Whale campaign, including an analysis of how this affected U.S.–Japanese relations. What was especially amusing was that Alex's friend Wendy was on hand, playing some normal six-year-old's game with Alex, and when her friend launched into this sophisticated discussion, Wendy looked at her, utterly baffled, as if spirits or demons had suddenly infested Alex.

Whenever possible, Alex would throw in big words: "Oh, Mother"—for some reason, she always preferred the more formal title for Carol, while reserving the diminutive for me—"you look so attractive tonight, just positively glamorous."

Telephones confound most children, like Chris. They are so taken in by the apparatus, the mechanical marvel, that it throws them off, and they are intimidated nearly to speechlessness. On the phone, for example, Chris rarely used anything but the word *good*. "How are you, Chris?"

"Good."

"How's everything at school?"

"Good."

"How're your friends?"

"Good."

"Did you know the world is coming to an end?"

"Good."

But Alex, who never gave a hoot about *things*—how they worked or were spelled or how to keep them neat—never let the telephone get in the way of a good conversation. In fact, since it made her grown-up on the one hand and encouraged imagining on the other, she was more than comfortable with the device and always conducted long, intelligent conversations with it. Then, as soon as she put the receiver down, she would toddle off, a five-year-old little girl again, sucking on the same corner of her little pink "blankie," clasping her Cher doll.

Anyway, while we were in Japan and Hong Kong, Alex dictated a couple of letters to us through Tina. They showed a normal preoccupation with missing us, but also an unusual fear that we might be harmed. Here is the first one:

> Dear Mother and Daddy,
>
> You are darlings and I love you. I hope you are having a good rest and a nice vacation. I hope God takes care of you and brings you home safely. My room is tidy. It really is. I did my chores, and I love you.
>
> Alex

Separation from us never troubled Chris so much, but perhaps Alex heightened his anxieties that one time. By chance, she had a difficult spell, coughing up a lot of mucus—what she always called "yukky," a very apt word that she borrowed from *Sesame Street*. Also, Chris caught on that Tina was familiar with cystic fibrosis and he asked her a lot of questions he had never asked Carol or me, or that he had nervously deflected whenever we had tried to bring the subject up with him. Where does this disease come from? How long will Alex have to do therapy? What would happen if she stopped taking her medicines? How come I didn't get it? That sort of thing.

That Sunday afternoon, Tina sat down at my typewriter to tell us some of this. "Christian is a child caught between the emotions of an eight-year-old and having the fragile understanding of what life is about. He becomes, even transcends, Alex's struggle: supportive, loving, the tender snuggling with her during her therapy to comfort and soothe; the

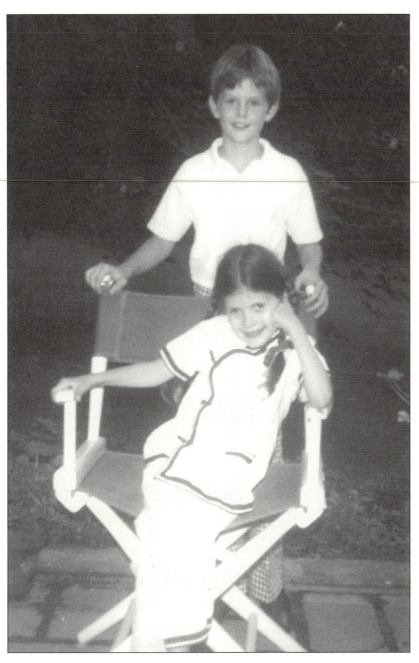

Big brother looking after little sis. This would have been the summer of 1976 or 1977.

wave of concern when she starts coughing; his gaze attends all her movements then, and his eyes say how much he'd like to do so much for her. His relationship with Alex is not just as a brother in the ordinary sense—there is no fighting, no picking on her—just a word now and then to knock her down. But then, he is the first to pick her back up."

Exactly as Tina was writing this, she heard noises and a commotion down the street. A neighborhood high school senior, Jeff Brown, who was especially well known to Chris because his brother Marc was one of Chris's best friends, had come around a corner too fast on his new motorcycle and slammed into a tree. Tina ran out, and the boy literally died in her arms.

Naturally, this affected both children greatly, although in different ways. Jeff's death made Chris face that subject for the first time. He was confused and despairing. Tina went back to my typewriter the next day and wrote: "Chris sobbed in our arms all afternoon and evening. He asked me: 'But where does life go? What happens when someone dies?' We talked about God, heaven, and souls. Then Christian said: 'You know, the saddest thing is that Jeff was too young to die. It goes so fast. All I can do now is remember Jeff.' "

For Alex, the death at first served mainly to increase her fears for us. She dictated,

> Dear Mother and Daddy,
> I am going to have a nap now, and I am sad you aren't here with me. I talked to Grandmother on the phone yesterday. I drew you a beautiful picture of a tulip.
> Jeff is in heaven and I am sad about that.
> I am frightened that you will be hurt, too. Please God, bring you back to me safely.
> Love,
> Alex

But the next day, more composed since some time had passed after the tragedy, Alex approached Tina in a much more analytical way, "Was it peaceful for Jeff?" she asked.

Tina said yes, he had showed no pain. And then Alex said, "It wasn't scary for you, was it?"

"No, it wasn't, Alex."

"Okay," Alex said. That was all. It was as if she were probing into what death would be like—not only for her, but also for those she left behind.

CHAPTER 15

And so we lived, Alex lived. Up early, inhalation and therapy in front of the TV. Television was diverting and made the time more tolerable, although seldom would Alex agree with Carol or me on what we should watch during therapy. Later on, at evening therapy, quiz shows proved to be something of a happy medium—if they put a gun to your head would you choose *The Joker Is Wild* or *The Gong Show?*—but mostly Alex's choices lay between uplifting children's fare—*Sesame Street, The Electric Company, The Magic Garden*—and adult junk reruns, notably *I Dream of Jeannie* or *Gilligan's Island*. It would be a besmirching of Alex's memory to reveal which of the two categories she preferred.

Alex also learned a lot of commercials while doing therapy, and sometimes (subconsciously, I hope) she even began to speak in that mock-serious tone that deep-throated announcers often employ. I remember, when she was about five or six she walked around for days, declaring—*declaring*—"Love goes on forever," much as some golden-throated shill on TV would exclaim: "Wondo is longer lasting."

Sometimes, of course, we would do the therapy without TV, just talking or perhaps listening to records. After Alex saw *Annie* we bought her the cast album, and pretty soon she had virtually the whole score memorized. Alex would sing it

107

all with a child's battery microphone—or "mokraphone," as she always called it.

Often during therapy Alex and I just chatted, too, so I imagine we spent more time talking during therapy than many fathers and their young daughters ever do. Once, as I was pounding on her, I idly asked Alex what she wanted to be when she grew up. She answered—and rather quickly, obviously having mulled this over before: "A princess."

"Hey, that's a good choice," I said. "Fine career. Good working conditions, terrific fringe benefits. Real nice line of work." And then I turned Alex into the next position, sideways, and started pounding another part of her chest.

The conversation soon left my mind, but, a few months later when we were doing therapy, Alex suddenly announced that she had thought about it some more, and, when she grew up, "I'd like to be Nadia Comaneci." This was, obviously, shortly after the 1976 Olympics; Alex was just turning five.

"Hey, that's a good idea," I said. "You'd be very famous, it would be healthy and exciting, and there'll certainly be an opening in that line by the time you grow up." She smiled, and soon I shifted her into a new position, one of the most uncomfortable ones, head down, as I pounded the sides of her chest. "But, Alex, why did you change your mind? The last time we talked about this you said you wanted to be a princess when you grew up."

"Well," Alex said, "I've thought about that, Daddy, and I decided I can't ever be a princess."

"Why?"

"Because I never heard of any princess having cystic fibrosis."

My heart bounced up into my mouth, but I managed to carry on. "Oh, look, Alex, I wouldn't worry about that," I said. "There're probably lots and lots of princesses, all over, who have cystic fibrosis, but you've just never heard about them. They probably just take their medicines and do their therapy so well that they're getting better all the time, so you don't hear about their CF."

She mulled that over for a few seconds, then shook her head. "No, Daddy, I just couldn't be a princess."

"Why?"

And this time she twisted her face up and around to look at me as best she could. And she said, "No, Daddy, I couldn't ever be a princess because my crown would fall off all the time whenever I did my therapy."

And she had me. I just returned to pounding her, trying not to cry out loud.

Then, each time after therapy came all the pills, the applesauce, the agonizing meals, pleading with her to take another bite—please just one more, half a bite, a nibble, anything. And, as Alex got older she would tire more easily, struggling to breathe, and we would try and get her to take naps. But often she fought that, too, because none of her friends took naps, and she didn't want to be different. More and more, and quite naturally as she grew older, Alex worried about being one of the girls. Going into the hospital always produced the additional concern that her friends would forget her while she was away.

Of course, and God bless them, it worked the opposite way. When Alex had to be hospitalized, the teachers always arranged class projects, everybody writing her cards and letters, taping messages to her, drawing her pictures, making up games for her. Then, when she did return, they welcomed her back with the truest affection. In the final couple of years, I would also make it a point on my visits to the hospital to take Alex down the hall, where she could call a school friend from the pay phones.

Alex's internal medications were kept in see-through plastic bags that hung from a pole, with the tubes going down into the needle stuck into her hand. The pole—we just called it her IV pole—was on a little stand, with rollers, so that she could be mobile and wheel it about the ward. Whenever I came to the hospital, I would have Alex step up on the little stand, a couple inches off the floor, and I would push her around. We'd go all over the ward, into the playroom, in to see her friends, and down the hall by the cafeteria to the pay phones, where she could call long distance back to Westport, to Wendy or Aimee, Robin or Tammie.

I don't care what excuses they give, it is sinful that hospitals don't figure out a way to let young patients' friends visit them—especially the kids who must go in regularly, or for long spells. Whatever infectious germs Alex might have picked up from her little pals would have been compensated a hundred times over by the psychological benefits such visits would have given her.

At midyear of her first-grade year, Mrs. Peggy Rabut, Alex's teacher, wrote this report. "Alex's plucky spirit is a fine example to all of us. Her cheery greeting each morning, her enthusiasm for all our projects and activities, and her willingness to help herself as much as possible are an inspiration. It is a privilege to have Alex in our midst."

Already, the kids, too, were beginning to understand how game Alex was, and how lacking in self-pity. A classmate who was far from being Alex's best friend wrote this to us after she died:

> This is what I remember of ALEX. Alex always smiled. Even if she was in pane. She always was nice to you. She meant so much to me and now she is gone. Gone till the day we die. She was always happy. And every day that she was alive was a bleasing. Alex was almost never frowning. She was never mean. She did not use her sickness to make people like her. Everone liked Alex because she was Alex. And she was so loveaboale. She made Many Happy Wishes.
> Carrie Wanamaker

110

Sometimes I think Alex cared so much for everything around her because she sensed that it was all she would have—that her elementary school would be junior high and high school and college, as well as her job, her husband, and her family—everything outside of the home she lived in for all her life. She embraced school with a passion, desperate to take it all in, pulling the others along as she did. After she died, Mrs. Rabut wrote us of that first-grade year:

> I feel very blessed to have been touched by Alex's life. The year she was in my class was probably the most memorable in my teaching career. It was a group of children who expressed love and consideration beyond what one normally expects from children of that age. There was a unifying force at work, and at the time, my only explanation was Alex. She commanded such respect on the part of her classmates by her determination to participate in every activity, to be as self-sufficient as possible, and to make the most of every minute of her day. We will all miss her—but in another sense, she will always be part of our lives—a shining example of courage, joy and hope.

Whatever it was, Alex threw herself into school, even, then, into arithmetic, which she couldn't get the hang of. With subjects that did interest her she was a tiger. If she heard me use a word, it wasn't enough for her to mimic it. "What's that word, Daddy?" *"Examine?"* "Yeah, what's that mean?" Then she would try it out. She brought the class guinea pig, Licorice, home for a week of vacation. She made "My Dinosoar Book"; studied a lot about prehistoric times; learned about geometric shapes, addition, and subtraction;

111

and especially enjoyed the social studies program, which examined family life.

Art was also a particular treat, and each month Alex would start off making a calendar, with some sort of appropriate drawing—a pumpkin for October, a turkey for November, and so on. February was my personal favorite: predictably red lettering, with predictably red hearts. Alex's hearts were too skinny, though. There is a widespread tendency when it comes to drawing hearts to make the two humps at the top first and then not to make the bottom part rounded enough. Alex was just like everyone else in that regard—she drew skinny hearts.

I did not, however, point this failing out when Alex brought the calendar home. But we always did talk a lot about what went on in school. Each day she'd hurry in to tell me what new activities were transpiring or show me something she had made. Sometimes, too, she would admit to slights she thought she had suffered, or to scholastic difficulties. But, whatever the travails, Alex was quick to recover. She was ever happy, and always, even in the midst of her own horrible, progressive agony, she thought of others. Every night Alex would say, "Now I lay me down to sleep," and she would conclude with her own litany of additional prayers. Eventually, it evolved pretty much into this set piece:

> Now I lay me down to sleep, I pray the Lord my soul to keep. If I should die before I wake, I pray the Lord my soul to take. And let nothing happen to God and Jesus and their angels. And Mary and Joseph [that was seasonally adjusted, for Christmas time]. And God, please take care of our country, and bring some of the poor people to our country, and make the other countries rich like us. And let someone find a cure for my disease, and all

the other diseases. And God, bless Mommy
and Daddy and Chrish and Chaucy."

And then she would kiss us, and smiling, snuggle up
to her favorite toy animal, a big, chunky lamb named Tink,
and go to sleep. Before long, Chris would leave his bed and
come in to join her.

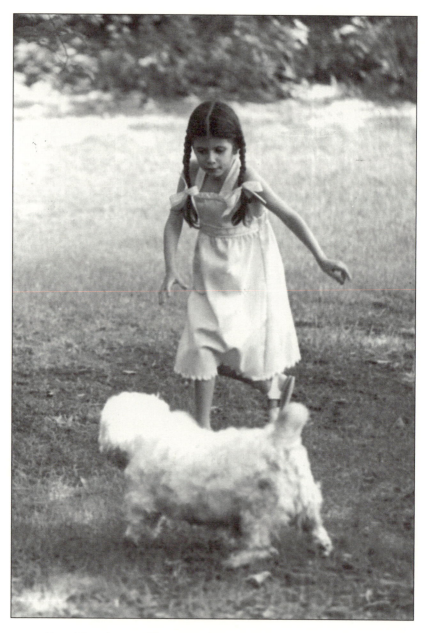

Alex giving chase to Chaucer in the backyard.

CHAPTER 16

On February 20, 1978, when Alex was going on six and a half, in the middle of the first grade, I wrote this:

"Alex went back to the hospital today. We had hoped so much that she could avoid that till the spring. She is the poster child in Connecticut for the Foundation and she has a big date in New Haven early in March with the Aetna World Cup. Aetna has made CF the official charity of the World Cup, largely because the Association of Tennis Professionals has honored the Foundation the same way—and that all came about because some of the tennis guys knew about Alex. So it really is her big time. She's going to get all dressed up and present the trophies, and she is already looking forward to the occasion—and the *exposure,* too! It's on TV, even if it is just public TV. But the most exciting other thing she's done as poster child is pose with a ninety-year-old man for a newspaper photo for a CF golf tournament, so this is a big step up.

"Also, just before the World Cup, we're all going down to Florida for a few days, where I'm working on a baseball story, and we certainly didn't want Alex to miss out on that, so we decided we better send her up to Yale–New Haven today, to get her regular ten-day treatment out of the way.

"Maybe it's just that we didn't have as much time to prepare ourselves for this hospitalization, as we usually do.

Maybe it's just that we're all down because it's the middle of an especially bad winter. Maybe it's just the accumulation of a lot of things. But, whatever, Alex's leaving upset Chris so much this morning, more than he ever would have let on in any traditional way. His behavior was so manic, so hyper—and it was even anti-Alex in some respects. That covered his fear, I guess.

"I think Chris well understands the implications of his sister's disease, even if he might never literally comprehend exactly what it means when I use the word *incurable*. Death is such a difficult concept for any child to deal with. But then, I suspect the same of Alex's own even-younger mind. If you told her flat out: Alex, incurable means this, that you are going to get worse and worse, there will be more pain and less of a normal life, and nothing—*nothing!*—can be done for you, and you must die very young without having a life to plan or knowing the simple joys of growing up in this world; well, if you told her all that, point-blank, and drove it home, she would surely break up on the spot.

"But the thing is, I know that she already knows all that. Yes, she senses it quite well, I'm sure—and then she goes on, managing nonetheless, somehow filtering only some of that comprehension into her everyday mind.

"Now, we've known all along that soon enough there would be one more major step down for Alex, but when it does happen, you are never prepared for the harshness of the inevitable. So it is now. And what madness, too. Now get this: the problem this time was signaled by Alex bleeding internally from doing her therapy. The bleeding itself was really not so bad, so crucial. It was just some little vessels bursting some-where because of all the pounding. But it means that for the vessels to heal, for no more of them to burst, we wouldn't be able to do the therapy. And if we can't do the therapy, the mucus will settle and collect, and the goddamned pseudomonas will spread.

116

"And here is the extra irony: As soon as we stopped doing the therapy, Alex started putting on weight. Talk about insanity. This cursed disease is the Devil's own, and all the worse for me that it is my child who has it and not me.

"When Alex first bled the other day, it scared her so. *Blood!* And honestly, even I wasn't prepared for that. As sophisticated as she is, too, in these matters, I didn't know whether she was only a little girl for the moment—*Blood! My blood!*'—or whether she was merely frightened that it was something new and unpredictable that she had to contend with. We had not prepared her for blood. Nobody had told us to look out for blood.

"The next day Alex told me that she was convinced this must mean the beginning of the end of her cystic fibrosis. 'How's that?' I asked. 'Well,' she explained, 'the blood had obviously replaced the yukky, and tomorrow or the next day, there would just be spit to replace the blood.' Spit is what she said. Spit. I tried to tell her, as gently as I could, that I hadn't heard anything about that and possibly that wasn't the case, and she nodded, sadly. It had seemed like a good idea. Then I went away to cry.

"Carol bought Alex a new dress for Valentine's Day. It's white with red trim. Alex adored it and wore it constantly. Then, a couple of days ago, she had it on and she was parading all about the house with her 'mokraphone,' singing and dancing. That was when the blood came up again.

"She called out. It was a horrible yell. I was in my office, and it pierced me. I jumped up and ran to Alex, but Carol had already reached her. I stopped in my tracks. The blood was all over, worse than it had ever been. Alex had dropped her mokraphone and was catching the blood in her hands, crying in fear, shaking.

"This destroyed Carol more than anything that has happened before. Oh, she was very controlled with Alex, very nurselike. She took care of the situation, calmed Alex down, even made sure to get her into another bright new dress-up dress, wipe the blood off the mokraphone, and give her that back. Alex didn't have the heart for that anymore, though, and only went off to her room with her dolls. So Carol came in to see me. I was just staring out the window at the snow—the white snow, like a white dress without blood on it.

"Carol was near tears now, but there was more anger than sadness. 'This beautiful little thing,' she said—and she snapped that off. 'This beautiful, gorgeous child in her Valentine dress, spitting up blood.'

" 'I know.'

" 'My God. My baby, spitting up blood.'

"I don't remember what I did. I only know that it wasn't much. I didn't know what to do. I only knew I must try and be strong and cool, for to go along with Carol would only make it seem all the worse. I did not know how to help her, I did not know what to do for her. And if I could not help her then, at that moment, then how will I ever be able to comfort anyone, ever, in my life? But that is the way this thing is. So all I can do is keep on thinking about Alex, about what a brave, majestic little thing she is. Just her; never mind me or Carol or Chris or anybody else. Still, beyond that, there must be some way for us to honor life through the prism of her meaning."

CHAPTER 17

The last really big birthday party Alex had was her seventh, on October 30, 1978, in the autumn of her second-grade year. She always had great birthday parties, because she was born the day before Halloween, and everybody had costumes on hand and was ready for a good time. Chris pointed out to me, on this occasion, that Halloween and Valentine's Day would make better holidays from school than some of the "boring" ones we officially have, and I agreed with him.

For her party Alex looked terrific, really smashing, in a brown dress with white trim, her hair caught up in a bun. Very sophisticated. She was quite the little coquette now, flirting shamelessly with me all the time. She even invited her two favorite boys to her party. One was Jonah, Tina Crawford's son, who was too close a family connection to be a certified love interest; the other was Stephen Baker, who was always identified as "my boyfriend," even though I never did quite get Stephen's intentions clear.

But never mind Stephen. Alex looked like a knockout to me, on this, her seventh birthday. Her face was fashionably thin, still quite beautiful. In the photographs of that day you have to look deep into her eyes and know what you are searching for to see what is there, to guess what is coming. I remember so well taking those pictures. Chaucer was hanging around, so we posed

Alex has a good laugh at her seventh birthday party. She is flanked by Wendy and Aimee, while Carol and her mother look on in the background.

Alex with him. He's a Sealyham terrier, and he had been a very frisky fellow who could sit up on his rear end just as easy as you please, and for minutes at a time (as long as he thought food was in the offing). But he was eleven years old then, too old to cut that kind of mustard anymore. Besides, Chaucer had a bad habit of going out in the street, so he got run over every now and again, which also cut down on his hijinks. Carol had hit him the year before in the driveway, on his birthday.

But he was still so cute, a picture-book dog, and it was a matching picture-book autumn day, so we posed Alex with Chaucer, amid the glorious leaves. And then, just as I

120

prepared to push the button again, very casually Alex said, "Just a second, Daddy. I have to cough first."

And she took a long time doing that, embarrassed at the fuss she caused. Understand, Alex wouldn't just cough. It would turn into a horrible gag, going on and on, as the mucus blocked her breathing. This happened more and more often, every day. She hated it so. After she died, one of her friends, Maura Frigon, wrote us: "Alex did not use her sickness to have people like her. Whenever she coughed someone would go get her a tissue. And whenever she coughed the class would say are you all right and she would say I'm all right."

Alex coughed an extra special large amount at her party that day because she laughed a lot. Carol had fixed up the most incredible bunch of fun and games, one with strings running all around, like a giant spiderweb. To get the prize, the children had to take their own string and go under it and around it and everywhere. But by then, whenever Alex enjoyed herself the most and laughed, she coughed. That was the damnedest irony of them all, that her greatest joys could trigger the worst inside of her.

This is what another classmate wrote to us about Alex:

> When Alex and I were riding in my mother's car going to the Beardsley Park Zoo on a Nursery School class trip and she was coughing so much my mother kept calling back to her to see if she was okay and Alex was trying to make my mother feel better.
> Sincerely,
> Emily S. Girard
> P.S. The capital "S" stands for Susan.

One day, when I was away, Wendy and Alex were drawing pictures in my office, and when Alex left the room,

Wendy took another piece of paper, and with the crayons, she wrote this, and left it for me.

> *The life about Alex Deford*
> By Wendy
> Alex Deford has a duzes but she is the kindest
> and nice little girl.

And she also drew a picture of Alex sitting in a chair.

Actually, Alex seldom wanted to be Alex at that time. She went through a phase when she wanted to be "Alexandra." Occasionally she would even take the effort to sign herself the complete Alexandra. She could write script by then. Here are some of the things that Alexandra wrote, in the second grade, at Brownies, or in the hospital. Generally you can tell the ones she wrote at the hospital because they appeared, corrected, in the ward newspaper.

> [The italics indicate form questions.]
> Once upon a time there lived a flower. She was very sad. [Picture of sad flower with blonde hair.] But then she saw a handsome man. [Happy flower with mustachioed handsome flower.]
>
> *What would you wish to be?*
> I wish I was a kitten in a buttrcup. Alex Deford
> *When do you feel good?*
> I feel good about myself when I help someone and there happy about it.
> Alex Deford
>
> I went to Williamsburg. I saw the colonel pepl. I saw the Guvinr's palis. I saw the black-Smith. I saw a lady macing wigs. I saw the

122

capitl where they made the laws. ladys wor long dress with howps. I like them.

My position in the family. I'm the littlest one in my family. I don't like being the littlest because I have to go to bed earlier than my brother who is ten years old.

Sometimes I like to play with my dolls and pretend that my dolls are smaller than me. [I never understood that, and forgot to ask Alex to explain it to me. I think if I had, she would have made up an answer, the way kids always do about their inexplicable drawings.]

My Christmas List
I what som new dress.
I what som books.
I what some games
I what some ballet posters
I what some jewelry.
I what some mariyonhets
I what some long undrwear
I what som scarves
Love Alexandra

I woke up and I was twelve feet tall. I got out of bed and broke through the ceiling. Then I couldn't find any clothes that fit me. So I took my sheet off my bed and wrapped it around me. It was a nice view out of the roof of my house.

What are you thankful for?
I am thankful for me and every things Around me. [The accompanying picture was the better part of this, showing a little girl,

123

obviously Alex, with a cartoon balloon coming out of her mouth. It said: "I love me."]

ALL ABOUT ME.

The Other Me. What Do you do when you're not in school?

I like to dance and sing and put on shows for my Mom and Dad.

I think a good friend should be [and here were the choices]:

cute   funny   rich   nice

[Alex had underlined *nice*.]

Why?

Who whants a mean friend.

Thinking Ahead.

What will I be when I'm 23?

I'll be a scientist and I'll be a enveter and go to the moon.

What will I be when I'm 43?

I'll see other children growing up and seeing new things.

What will I do when I'm 62?

I'll chat on the phone a long, long time like my Nana does.

If I'm alive at 95 . . .

They'll have new inventians. I'll sit in my old rocking chair.

WHEN I'M GROWN UP I hope I will be:

1.—a dancer
2.—a singer
3.—actress
4.—pritty
5.—rich
6.—smart.
7.—good grades

You get THREE WISHES! Think carefully.
This could change your life.

1. I wish I could have a cure for my disease.

[Dutifully, Alexandra also put down two other wishes.]

CHAPTER 18

One day, as it turned out, almost exactly a year before Alex died, Carol took her into New York. It was a very special occasion, because Alex was one of two cystic fibrosis patients appearing in a television commercial. She didn't have to do much—there were no lines for her—but she loved being a real genuine certified actress—in New York, near Broadway, no less!—and she played very well to the crowds.

The commercial was shot downtown, in Washington Square, and then Carol took Alex to lunch at a little restaurant in Greenwich Village. Even if Alex didn't care much about eating, she loved to go to restaurants—the fancier the better. Afterward they went uptown to Central Park and the zoo. It was a brisk day, but bright in the sun, and comfortable if you could keep moving along with someone you loved.

"It was a very special day—the commercial and all that," Carol told me later. "And I guess looking back, that it was the last day like that Alex and I ever had. A whole day treat together, a trip somewhere, just the two of us. So I remember it especially vividly. No, it wasn't the last 'good' day she had, but it's one I can visualize so clearly because it was so special. Alex was at her cutest, her cheeks all red, her hair in the braids I loved. We walked a lot, downtown, all over the zoo. *Walked!* I remember that so clearly. She was still able to walk some."

In only a few months, though, by May, the final decline had really set in. That was when Cyd Slotoroff first met Alex. Cyd never saw anything but the worst. There was not much to the last eight months of Alex's existence except pain and doubt. How Alex kept going, without losing faith and love, is the greatest wonder of her life. Sometimes I think that she was kept alive as long as she was to prove all that she was.

A few months after Alex died Cyd wrote a song called "Child of the Stars." When she introduces it at concerts, she says, "I'm privileged to work with kids in a hospital. I've learned a lot from many of these children, but one little girl I met taught me more about life than anyone, and this is for her." And then Cyd sings:

Child of the stars,
I know you're free now.
Child of the stars,
You came and you're gone now,
Gone to a new home—
You didn't stay long.

Peace in your eyes,
You saw with your heart.
Gentle and wise,
Drew lightness from dark,
Opening, though knowing soon
You'd be called away.

And I, I carry you on
In my heart and in my song.
You are shining true,
You are shining through me . . .

That May of 1979, when Cyd first met Alex, she was only beginning to die. Alex had to stay in the hospital over Memorial Day, and I was away on an assignment, so Carol went up to Yale–New Haven for the hospital's holiday picnic. It was a real picnic, too. Except for the few children who were attached to machines, they managed to get all the kids outside on the lawn. There were balloons, party food, and clown makeup, and the local television station had a crew come over and get everybody on tape for the evening news. Alex was in sort of a wheelchair, Cyd was playing her favorite songs and the kids were singing along, but Alex barely raised her head, even when Cyd sang something like "Ship in the Harbor," which she adored. Alex was still coming to grips with the fact that, despite it all, she had declined to another, lower level.

Always before, no matter how poorly off she was when she came into the hospital, Alex could be revived by the ten days there, by the rest and antibiotics. But this time she had to stay in for at least an extra week, and so many new things had gone wrong that it was impossible for her to be restored. Along with all the usual ailments involving her lungs and pancreas, Alex also began to suffer from a weakened heart, liver problems, arthritis, regular high fever, and pneumonia. There was so much wrong that some things just got lost in the shuffle. Various medicines would cause Alex uncomfortable (and unattractive) chapping around her lips, the sort of ailment that would normally make parents alarmed and solicitous. God forgive me, I can actually remember being short with Alex once when she brought the subject up. It was like her old complaints about applesauce, almost as if she didn't have the right to bitch about a relatively minor ailment the way everyone healthy did.

Or, to put it in perspective, and in her own terms, one day the next fall, when Alex was sicker still, she'd somehow managed to escape the hospital for a few days and come back

129

to her school. Her class was going somewhere, marching down the hall—the way all third-graders everywhere march down the hall—but Alex fell quickly behind. Mrs. Beasley dropped back to offer her some help, but Alex only shook her head and apologized that she had caused all this attention. "I'm sorry," she said, "it's just my arthritis."

I don't know how she carried on. I doubt that she ever topped forty pounds. I don't see how a person so thin could have the room to have so much wrong inside.

By then, the hospital was a second home. There were all those other little children, in tents, with tubes, hooked up to machines, heads shaven, limbs gone; and their parents staring out, numbed, baffled, scared, so utterly helpless. Depending on the patient population, Alex would be given her own room, share a semiprivate, or be put in a four-bed dormitory. When she was placed in with other children, I always hoped that the kid next to her would be Hispanic, with parents unable to speak English well, so that I wouldn't have to try and converse with them. The trouble was that I so envied—or despised—those lucky parents whose children were only in for a day or two, for some accident or minor operation.

I think, in fact, that the closest I ever came to committing homicide was a night in the hospital that last May. A little girl was brought in to share a room with Alex. She had a dog bite, so she had been brought in for observation, overnight. A foolish little dog bite, one night—and her mother was moaning and whining about this calamity, and worst of all, about what a rotten hospital it was because her poor daughter couldn't rent a television set *right away.*

Alex told the woman not to worry, she would be delighted to share her set, and that calmed things down for a moment. "What's your little girl in for?" the woman asked me, in that tactless way some adults do, talking about a child in front of her instead of talking to the child.

"She has cystic fibrosis," I said.

"Oh yeah, I've seen all those telethons with Jerry Lewis," she replied airily. I didn't bother to correct her. I just walked away. I had to get out. I went down to a little Puerto Rican store on the corner and bought a cigar. I don't know why; it had been years since I smoked cigars.

When I came back, the little girl with the dog bite and her mother had pretty much commandeered Alex's TV set, so I took Alex out of bed, got her to stand on the base of her IV pole, and pushed her down to the playroom where we could be by ourselves. There we talked about the wonderful summer we would have after she got out of the hospital. Chris was going off to a camp for a couple weeks, so I promised Alex that her mother and I would take her somewhere then—just the three of us. She beamed at that; she really looked especially adorable then, because she had lost her two front teeth, like any seven-year-old. But then, quickly she grew very solemn.

"What's the matter?" I asked.

"Chrish won't mind, will he, Daddy?"

"Oh, no," I said, and I went on to reassure her, telling her all the special things he would be doing at his camp and with his grandmother and grandfather, with whom he would be spending the nights. Of course, all the while, in the back of my mind, I kept thinking about how, soon enough, it would only be Chris and Carol and me, *that* three of us, all the time.

That was the first night I had real difficulty driving back from the hospital. It was normally about a thirty-five-minute trip from New Haven to our house, and after a while I sort of did it on automatic pilot, but this night it was hard for me to drive at all. Finally, I had to pull over because I was crying so hard I couldn't drive safely. When I finally managed to get myself home, I went to my typewriter and wrote:

"Poor, dear Alex is so much worse. The decline has been swift. I would know that simply from the way the nurses talk to me now. Alex realizes herself, too, if only because she is in pain so much of the time. When she comes home, whenever, she'll have to sleep with an oxygen device, prongs stuck into her nose, and already I wonder whether prolonging her life is worth it from here on. I would guess she has another year or so, maybe even two, but she is so weak now that her life has become precarious. Could she survive any new crisis today? I doubt it.

"I am down to hoping for a miracle now, and I know Carol understands that, too. She has been so depressed lately, and now the summer is coming. The summers always seem to be the worst for her, when she doesn't have school and schoolwork to escape to. Then it just seems that she never gets away from it, that cystic fibrosis simply overwhelms her. Last summer was practically the ruin of us. We'll have to try even harder to make the best of this one.

"Alex and I discussed the tooth fairy tonight, and inflation vis-à-vis that particular occupation. Of course, she's very tooth conscious now, without hers. Gee, she's so cute. And still, through it all, she continues to trust in the beauty of life. What is this child made of that she can be robbed of everything but pain, and yet sit there and laugh with me about the tooth fairy?

"I suppose that is why, if it is just a matter of keeping her alive, I would be hard-pressed to want her to struggle on. Or am I only being selfish when I think that? Do I just want this awful thing resolved so that I can drive a car without crying again, so that I can find some peace, so that I can get on about my life? I don't know. God, I don't. I only know one thing for sure, that we have had this extraordinary little creature with us for seven years of joy, and I fear it must only be all diminishing returns from here on in. I think it would be best for God to take her now, while she can still dwell on the tooth fairy."

• • •

But there were some things about the hospital that made Alex feel comfortable and assured. Cyd coming by to sing and play was the highlight of any day. She could make Alex joyful, almost no matter how bad she felt. Cyd would often use Alex as a critic, trying out her new children's songs on her first. Cyd tried out a happy little number called "One of a Kind" on Alex, and she liked it so much that Cyd wrote a couple extra verses especially for her.

Lots of the time, too, Cyd would play the more traditional songs; "She'll be Comin' 'round the Mountain" was a special favorite. Alex would always request that when I was visiting, because she knew I would insert some really risqué verses—like "She'll be skinny-dipping when she comes"—and Alex would absolutely break up at that, delightfully embarrassed that I was saying such things in front of Cyd. But then one last time this brought out the worst in Alex and suddenly she got giggly and foolish and made up verses like "She'll be picking her nose when she comes" or "She'll be going to the bathroom when she comes." It reminded Cyd and me that Alex was still just seven years old and could be like any seven-year-old when she wasn't dying. Or maybe, as Cyd suggested, Alex was somehow trying to escape into silliness.

Another treat was an intern who would come by on his off-hours as a volunteer a couple of nights a week and make balloon animals for the kids. His real name was Steven Brown, but to everyone he was, simply, the Balloon Man. There were also some wonderful ladies who came week after week to run the craft room, and there were several others known as "grandmas," who just came and provided company for the kids—especially those whose parents couldn't visit much. Mornings there were school and other projects for the patients. The ward newspaper, mimeographed irregularly, was known as the Fitkin 5 *Globe*. Alex had named the paper during one of her earlier visits. They were searching for a name, so Alex asked me for some suggestions, and then she settled on *Globe* because she knew a few kids there had come from far-off places. "I think this will make them think it is more their newspaper, too," she said.

Alex adored most all the nurses. There was Florine and Maribeth, Pat, Debbie, Judy, Joanne, Sue, Wanda, and Stephanie, the receptionist. Barbara, her best pal among the nurses, says, "Alex always accepted things so well. She only lived eight years, but she mastered life much better than most of us. She could cope with anything they threw at her . . . well, except maybe the needles. But she always had such a wonderful humor, and that's why we all loved her."

And Cyd again: "Alex really was a wise old soul—such wisdom for her years—but she was also so generous and thoughtful. You could always tell it came right from the heart. I can't quite say she became a legend, but I can say this: There are certain children, a few, in any children's ward, who are remembered. Alex was one of those. There have been times I've brought up Alex's name, and some new nurse, who never knew her, will say, 'Oh yeah, I've heard all about Alex.' She was that special."

The nurses, of course, were the more permanent cadre. The residents and interns, like the patients, would come and go. In fact, it was rather like the army, where even if a fuzzy-faced new lieutenant holds officer's rank, he will often as not defer to the grizzled old sergeant. Unfortunately, sometimes a kid doctor would run roughshod over the nurses, and they would have to take it. After a while, after Alex had established a certain amount of tenure herself, she didn't like any rookie in a white smock bossing her around, and she would stand up to him if she felt she had to.

Once an especially officious young resident came into Alex's room to change her IV from one hand to the other. Alex abhorred this procedure under the best of circumstances, and she did not at all like what he was suggesting. Without mincing words (so a nurse who was there told me) Alex advised the kid doctor that she had been taking IVs for a long time—she didn't possess quite enough sophistication to add *longer than you've been dishing them out, pal.* But she made the point well enough—that he better get it straight: IVs were only given in the treatment room. The kid doctor said he was sorry, but that the treatment room was in use right now, so they would have to make do with her own room.

Alex then said, no, wait till the treatment room is free. The resident said there wasn't time and started approaching her.

Alex drew back on her bed. "No!" she screamed. "This is my room! This is my bed! You don't have any right to hurt me in here." And then she began to cry.

The nurse then stepped in, drew the young doctor aside, and counseled him to go along with Alex, which, at last, he grudgingly agreed to do. He cooled his heels till the treatment room was free and he could change Alex's IV there.

Alex told me herself about this episode that night. "Wasn't I right, Daddy?" she asked me, and I assured her that she was.

Then, the next day, unable to write because the IV had been shifted to the right hand, Alex dictated this editorial to Nancy Wallace, who ran the Child Life Program, which put out the Fitkin 5 *Globe*.

> There is a room where you have an IV done, the Treatment Room.
>
> Having your own room, with friends, it's the thing in the hospital that's like your own home. It's a place for you to stay, and lie down and sleep. It can be nice and comfy.
>
> If you have an IV there or even a finger stick, then it doesn't feel like you're even at home!

Only getting your IV taken out in your
own room is really okay.

I wish they would post this message for residents and
interns in children's wards everywhere.

.

CHAPTER 19

Alex finally did get out of the hospital and was able, officially, to finish the second grade, but by then she was so far behind that we started having Marlayne Schaeffer, who had been Alex's dance teacher, come in and tutor her. Alex was, as ever, conscientious, but it was growing harder for her to sustain any effort.

"Sometimes," Marlayne remembers, "she was obviously just so tired, but other times I came to realize that she was only being gracious when she said that, that she was really just in great pain, but didn't want to burden me with that knowledge."

By then, even when Alex was not, for the moment, sick, we were on edge, poised, never far from trauma. Every day there was a crisis atmosphere, for she would so often plan something simple—to go see a movie, to have a friend visit— and it would have to be canceled at the very last minute because she showed a high fever. Sometimes I thought that, no matter how many ways she could get sick, it would be a broken heart that would kill her. By then the emotional deprivations were growing as great as the physical.

As I promised, we did go away together, the three of us. When Chris went off to camp, we went to a little hotel in Kennebunkport, on the Maine coast. Then, one day late in the summer, Alex and I went into New York together, hung out, got some ice cream, and went to *The Muppet Movie*. That was to be the last time the two of us did anything really special together. But there were a couple times during the summer when Alex was well enough to be able to have a friend over to spend the night with her. However, sadly, she was never well enough at the right time to have Wendy and Aimee come together for a sleepover. They had done that occasionally in the past, all three of them jammed into Alex's bed.

There was one especially memorable night that Aimee wrote about after Alex died. "This is what I remember about Alex. When me and Wendy slept over. We were so tired and squished that me and Alex pushed Wendy to the end of the bed. We got to sleep for a while and then woke up and me and Wendy did commercials. Alex was cracking up. Then we got to sleep. Well that was a time to remember."

Alex remembered it, too, right to the end. In fact, a few days before she died she told me about that night—about the commercials and fashion shows and everything, and she said, "You know, that was the happiest night I ever had, Daddy." Then quickly, so as not to hurt my feelings, she added, "I mean, outside my little family."

But as the summer wore on the pain increased, and Alex had to be denied so much that even her spirits began to flag. A few months before, she had initiated a conversation about the general subject of illnesses, why some people get them and others don't. Till then, that was about as close as she had ever come to cursing her luck. But even then she hadn't approached the matter directly. Instead, the question she posed was, "What is the worst disease in the world?"

We discussed the matter for a while. On the one hand, I didn't want to give Alex's disease short shrift and make light of what she suffered; but, on the other hand, neither did I want to make cystic fibrosis sound so bad that it would depress her. Finally, we came to an agreement that the worst disease of all would be one that left you completely paralyzed. There had been a little boy from South America in Yale–New Haven who could hardly move anything but his eyelids, and he obviously had left a great impression on Alex. "Don't you think that would be the worst?" I asked.

She thought for a time, and nodded. But then, very quickly she looked directly at me. "Then what's the second worst?" she asked.

I couldn't walk any more tightropes that day. "Well, what do you think, Princess?"

"Oh, I think I know," she said, and she only smiled at me, for trying to be kind.

By the summertime, though, Alex no longer felt she had to be evasive about such matters. She had more pain all the time and hated the nose prongs that she had to sleep with now, to get more oxygen. By August it was obvious that she would soon have to go back to the hospital, and, in fact, we postponed it for a week or so to allow her to make the first day of third grade.

There was a point beyond which even Alex's goodwill was tested, and that came to be reached regularly, especially when we did therapy. Obviously, no one enjoys being turned this way and that, upside down and sideways, for an hour or more every day, while somebody pounds on her, but Alex was as good at accepting that as anyone you could imagine. When she did complain, it was more in the nature of any kid trying to get away with something, like Chris asking why he had to eat carrots or why he couldn't stay up later. So it was: Why do we have to do therapy now? Can't we skip this one? Let's finish it later. But really for the first time in any sustained way, that summer Alex began to complain about the very nature of the therapy. Soon almost every time she was screaming at Carol or me. "You're hurting me, Mother!" "Please, Daddy, stop now, please, please. This hurts!"

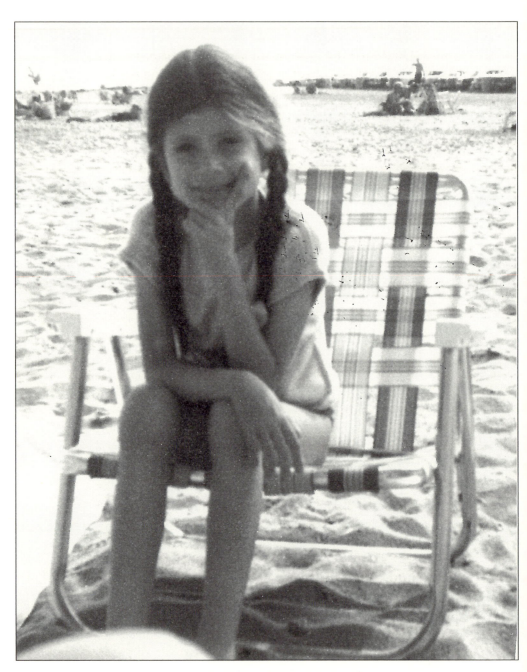

Alex's last summer, at the beach in 1979, right in Westport. I really love her expression here.

When I did the therapy, she would call me names and tell me that Carol did a better job. When Carol did it, Alex would tell her that *she* was the torturer. But worst of all, I think, was this conversation:

"Can't we stop it, Daddy?"

"Let me just finish, Alex."

"But it hurts me. Please, please."

"I'm sorry, Alex, but I have to."

"All right. Why?"

"You know, to help you."

"I don't think so anymore."

"You don't think what?"

"You know, Daddy. It isn't helping me, is it?" I didn't say anything. "Is it?" she asked, and harshly.

"Of course it is," I lied the best I could. To be truthful, I wasn't sure anymore that the therapy did help much, and if it did, so what if it took so much pain to accomplish only a little?

When we finally told Alex that she would have to go back in the hospital right after school started, she fell to still lower depths. Carol took her out and bought her some new clothes, but it didn't help much. That was probably the worst time for Alex, because I believe now—looking back—that was when she finally came fully to grips with reality. She understood it all, at last. The only thing left was to play it out. I surely don't know myself, but I suspect that the hard part is to learn to embrace death, as Alex was doing in those months; it's easier, when the time comes, for death merely to embrace you.

But Alex was able to go to school that first day, and I was waiting at home when she got off the bus and began to struggle up the driveway. I ran out to meet her, and on the pretense of hugging her, picked her up and carried her the rest of the way in. Then we sat down and discussed all the things any parent would want to know about the first day of school: Where was your desk? How did you like your teacher? Did you meet any new friends? And Alex answered all the questions with the most incredible excitement and enthusiasm. Even in my most optimistic projections of her longevity, I doubted that she could possibly last out the school year, but here we were talking about a school year, about a grade, about a spring that would surely never come for her.

And yet Alex wanted and planned to be a part of her third grade. "Daddy," she said, "do I really have to go in the hospital tomorrow? Please."

"Oh come on, Alex, you—"

"I won't argue about my therapy. I promise. Please, don't make me."

"You're not being fair, Alex. You know you really were supposed to go in a few days ago, and we kept you out just so you could go to school today."

"I have to go?"

"Yes, Princess, you have to. Don't get mad at me."

She nodded then, and came over and sat in my lap. "Can I tell you something then?"

"Sure."

"But I don't think you'll like it."

"Well, try me."

"Okay. I've stopped praying, Daddy. I mean, I've stopped praying for a cure . . . a cure for my disease."

I didn't protest. I just shook my head in understanding. "I can see why."

"You can?"

"Sure. You're always way down in the dumps whenever you have to go back in the hospital. It's tough for you now. I know. Is it okay with you if I keep on praying?"

She hugged me and said that was all right. We held each other for a long time, then, and when I cried, I was quick to whisper to her that I was just so sad that she had to leave

142

her school and go back into the hospital. Finally, when she pulled away from me, she said, "Daddy, do you remember that time we talked about the worst disease of all?"

"Yeah, I remember."

"It's cystic fibrosis, isn't it?"

"Yeah, I guess it is," I said.

"I thought so," Alex said, and we both nodded and cried some more. "See, Daddy, I'd pray if I could see something, just something, but"—and just then she happened to glance down at her fingers gesticulating before her. "Oh, no, Daddy, look at my fingers now. They're even worser."

I took them and kissed them and held them, so that she wouldn't have to see them and be reminded.

"You know Crissy?" she asked after awhile.

"You mean the other little girl in the hospital with CF?"

"Yeah."

"Sure, I remember Crissy. She was nice."

"Do you think she'll be in the hospital this time, too?"

"Oh, I don't know, Alex. I just don't know."

"I think she probably will be," Alex said. "She's got this disease real bad, too. Me and Crissy have it worse, don't we? She has real bad fingers, too."

"Yeah, I know," I said. "Some kids with CF don't have it so bad. Some of them really just have problems with their stomachs."

Alex's eyes widened at that. I guess I'd never told her that before. "Oh, they're so lucky, Daddy," she said. "They're so lucky."

"Yeah," I said, agreeing that it sure was lucky just to be a little bit incurable.

"But I'll die," Alex said. It was the first time I had ever heard her say anything like that. And it was a statement, too. She had obviously worked this out so that she would be presenting the matter, not asking me about it.

"Well, sure," I said, as casual as I could be myself. I'd been prepared for this for a long time. "You'll die sometime. But I'll die, too. If there's one thing we all do, it's die."

"But you'll be real old," she said.

"Not necessarily. I mean, I could die in an accident anytime."

Alex threw her arms around my neck. "Oh, my little Daddy, that would be so unfair."

"Unfair?" I said. *Unfair* is just what she said.

"You don't have a disease, Daddy. You shouldn't have to die till you're real old." And then she hugged me as hard as she could.

As I held her I remembered a few weeks before when Carol and Alex and I had been in Maine together, the three of us. One evening we went out to a place on the rocks in Kennebunkport named Spouting Rock, where a natural cave has been formed with an opening at the top. When the water rushes into the cave, it whooshes up through the opening. Alex always got a big kick out of it.

We parked the car and I picked Alex up and carried her down the rocks, carefully negotiating my way, so that we could see Spouting Rock up close. It had still been clear when we got there, but as so often happens along the Maine coast, a fog suddenly rolled in, and then we could barely make out Spouting Rock.

I clambered back up the rocky slope with Alex and went over to where Carol was waiting. I sat down there with her, and looked out over the rocks toward the water. We could barely make it out anymore. Alex had asked me to put her down, and she stayed near the edge. She had on a shirt and pink shorts and sandals, her little knees sticking out, her hair in pigtails, a ribbon holding each, and she was skipping back and forth, waving to us, and even laughing for happiness except when she had to pause and cough.

Carol and Alex, probably in 1977.

Softly, Carol began to cry, watching her. I didn't say anything. Without ever talking about it, Carol and I had come to an understanding, that when one of us saw the other start to cry, there was no need to ask why or to try and offer solace. That would only make us both cry. And besides, so many times, as then, we didn't want to call Alex's attention to our grief. So we sat there, Carol crying, I staring.

In a few more moments it had become downright misty. There was no sky, no trees, no water, no house across the inlet. The only thing we could see, at any distance, was Alex, softly treading the rocks.

145

"My God, look at her," Carol whispered.

Suddenly, from nowhere three or four seagulls appeared. They swooped down, and then they headed off again, gliding toward the water, except hardly had they gone any distance at all before they were enveloped in the fog, and, like that, gone. Alex stopped to watch them disappear, and then walked toward us. "Did you see those seagulls?" she asked, and I said, "Yeah, weren't they something?"

"Did you see them, Mother?" Alex asked, and Carol nodded too, trying not to show her tears. Alex was just enthralled by the birds and the scene. She kept shaking her head, looking off to where they had gone.

"Wasn't that something?" she said. "Just to go like that. They just seemed to drift off, didn't they? It was like they just floated away."

And what both Carol and I thought often around that time and what I thought again as I held Alex, was that this would be the best way for her to go. The same sort of thought, this primitive imagery, stayed in Alex's mind, too, as I would find out. But for now, she had to leave her school and go back to the hospital.

CHAPTER 20

Fortunately, Alex was able to return to school in time for her class picture, which was taken one day late in September. Mrs. Beasley sat her smack in the middle of the front row, like the captain, with Jonah Crawford on one side and Jake Weinstock on the other. Aimee and Wendy were seated directly behind her.

In the picture Alex is wearing blue shoes, red tights, and a red dress, with red ribbons on her pigtails. Her two front teeth have come in most all the way, and she has the world's biggest, brightest smile. Of course, if you knew enough to look closely, you could see that her skin was chapped around her lips and her teeth discolored from the medication. But she looks pretty, and she loved the picture herself, which was all that mattered. It was the last one taken of her in which pain and death were not evident.

On October 11, Alex's lung collapsed.

This is not necessarily a crisis with most people. Athletes, at the peak of health, can have a lung collapse simply by overextending themselves. For them it is only a matter of more or less pumping it back up again. Only about 3 percent of cystic fibrosis patients ever suffer a collapsed lung, and the figure is even lower for those under the age of ten.

But Alex got the short stick again. I was away in Florida when it happened, and Carol rushed her up to Yale–New Haven. They had to make an incision in Alex's chest and stick a tube in.

We could never give Alex therapy again, as long as she lived.

It took a long time for the lung to heal, but Alex was able to come home at the end of October, and we had a quiet family birthday party. That made her eight years old. That Friday all four of us went into New York and saw *Peter Pan* on Broadway. That was Alex's big birthday present, and it was an excellent one; she adored it, and, as we might have expected, Alex could recite huge chunks of the show verbatim the next day.

Unfortunately, Alex was so weak that it wore her out just lasting through such a long day, and when we couldn't get a cab after the theater, I had to carry her for blocks. She hugged me around the neck after awhile and said, "Daddy, thank you for carrying me. I'm sorry."

"Hey, that's all right, Princess. This is your birthday. Anybody can get carried on their birthday. I might even carry old Christian on his."

And she laughed, gave me a kiss to go with the hug, and said, "Oh, this has been such a great birthday. I'm very lucky, because I know that not too many little girls would get to go to Broadway."

Alex was always weak from that point on. Mrs. Beasley had noticed it. "After the lung collapsed there was a discernible difference," she told me later. "A couple times I looked up and Alex had just put her head on her desk and dozed off." Still, Alex kept trying as hard as she could; she didn't ever want to be left behind or left out. And, as Jake Weinstock told his parents, no matter what happened, "Alex never used her disease." It was probably good for everybody around that she got back to school for a few days.

When she died, Jake's father, Davis Weinstock, wrote a lovely eulogy in the Westport paper for Alex, and a part of that tribute told of her effect upon her friends.

> Perhaps the primary recipients of Alex's gifts were the twenty-one other members of Mrs. Pat Beasley's third-grade class at Greens Farms Elementary School. With guidance from Mrs. Beasley, but with impetus entirely from within themselves, the class had undertaken projects of unusual scope and uncommon dedication. Some projects had to do with Alex: a tape with each of their voices serving as a newsletter; an elaborate sleigh constructed of cookie dough; signed scrolls, cards, goodies, and more. Other extensive projects were not for Alex, but evidenced the rare functional cohesiveness the class had learned to enjoy. These the class would share with Alex, by mail, by tape, by phone, by whatever means her circumstances dictated. Stronger forces than sympathy were at work: friendship and admiration. . . . Alex's schoolmates knew she hurt. She hurt a lot. But, of all the hurts, she only admitted to the one of staying behind at recess. She was a participant. By the testimony of her schoolmates, Alex was the child who "never frowned."

One day Aimee and Wendy showed the class what therapy was like, and they told the others more of the things Alex had to endure at home—difficulties she had never mentioned. The boys seemed to be impressed, in many ways, more than were the girls. By her example, Alex did a lot of consciousness raising.

149

The teachers suggested to Alex that it might be a good idea for her to go lie down on the school nurse's cot during recess. She didn't like the idea, but she couldn't play vigorously anymore, so she knew it was the sensible thing. But one day during recess, when Mrs. Beasley wanted to check with Alex about something, she couldn't find her in the nurse's office. She couldn't find her anywhere, and she started to get a little frightened. Finally, she located Alex in the gymnasium, with a lot of other kids. They were practicing singing for the Christmas pageant, and, tired as she was, Alex decided that she didn't want to miss out on that. So, somehow, she had struggled over to the gym, and when Mrs. Beasley came in, "There was Alex, standing up there so straight, singing with all the others."

At Halloween, Wendy and Aimee and Robin Oliver put on a play. They had written it when Alex was in the hospital, but it was inspired by a time they had played witch with Alex at our house. Fortunately, Alex was out of the hospital in time to present the play, and she happily volunteered to take the witch's role. All the other little girls wanted to play sweet little girls, but Alex could see a juicy scene-stealing role. She went around hunched over, rubbing her hands together, saying, "Heh, heh, heh, all my little sweeties," and brought the house down.

Alex was even able to go to Brownie meetings a couple times that fall. At one she gave a report on her personal favorites. Her favorite color, she said, was pink. Her favorite song was "Hopelessly Devoted to You," from *Grease*. "The best thing I like to do is dance," she wrote. Her favorite TV show was *Benny Hill*, the bawdy British music hall comedian, who does a lot of stuff in drag. Her favorite hobby was collecting glass animals. Her favorite stuffed animal was Tink, the big soft lamb her Great-Aunt Juliet had given her.

But then, soon enough, Alex and Tink had to go back to the hospital. Without therapy, her lungs were deteriorating

Alex playing at home.

faster, but we couldn't give her therapy without the probability of her lungs collapsing. And she desperately needed the IVs. "I'm afraid it's really short now," I wrote when she went back, early in November. "I don't believe she'll see the trees bloom again. I only fear that the lung will keep collapsing, and she will never get out of this damn hospital, and she will die there of a broken heart. All I want now is for her to be able to come home, have Christmas with us and die here in her own bed, surrounded by us and all the things she loves.

"How quickly our fool dreams change: just to have her back at home for a day is all I dare wish for now."

Alex already understood that her time was fading, and there was much she must do for herself. Late in September, just before her lung first collapsed, we had traveled to Baltimore to visit my parents and help celebrate my mother's birthday. It was a grand family occasion, because my brother Mac, who is Alex's godfather, was also there with his family, his wife, Zehra, and their little son, Benjie. This was extra special, because Mac was usually abroad. At the time he was a Foreign Service officer, and now he's with Merrill Lynch's international division.

He's been stationed in the far corners of the world: Jordan, Korea, Argentina, Vietnam; he met Zehra when he was posted to Jidda, Saudi Arabia. She's Turkish, and Alex was always especially taken by Zehra, who was exotic and sweet. And so on this trip to Baltimore, Alex cornered Zehra in her bedroom at my parents' house, while she was straightening up.

"Zehra," Alex said, "I want to ask you something."

"Yes, of course, what is it?"

"Is there a God?"

Zehra was, to say the least, staggered. Among other things, she's a Moslem, and the last thing she wanted was to start leading this little Christian astray. "Well, I think so," Zehra ventured.

"How do you know?" Alex asked.

"I don't know. I just feel sure there is. I talk to Him when I need Him."

"You do? How?"

"You know, Alex: praying."

"Oh," she said. "I do that, too. Do you think He'd listen to me?"

"I think He listens to everybody," Zehra said, and, nervously, she started puttering about again. Alex sat down on the floor and watched her for a while. Zehra didn't understand that Alex had carefully selected her for these questions. She was a good friend, and family, and Alex liked her, so she could ask Zehra questions she wouldn't dare ask Carol or me. After awhile Alex spoke again. "Zehra?"

"Yes, sweetheart?"

"How do you die?"

Zehra stopped her cleaning up and turned directly to Alex. She would deal directly, the best she could. "It's mostly just like going to sleep," Zehra said. "All of a sudden, though, you aren't in this house. You're in God's house."

"Where's that?"

"That's in Heaven."

Alex thought about that for a while. "Are there toys there?"

"Oh, yes, lots and lots."

"But it would be lonely without your family, wouldn't it?" Alex said. There was no doubt from the way she said that, that it would be lonely because she knew she would surely be going first.

"Oh, no, everyone will be there soon enough," Zehra said.

"You, too?" Alex said. "Mac and Benjie? Grandmommy and Granddaddy?"

"Everybody. But before they do get there, you can always look out through a window in Heaven and see everyone down here that you love and you miss."

"You can?"

"Sure you can, Alex. Or otherwise it wouldn't be Heaven."

Alex thought about that for a moment, and then she got up and thanked Zehra and left her there to finish cleaning up.

CHAPTER 21

The most maddening thing about being in a teaching hospital is that, at different times, six different groups of doctors and students will inspect you, asking the same questions over and over. The more times Alex had to go back to Yale–New Haven, the more irritated she grew at this sort of thing, because it was a nuisance, of course, and also because it suggested to her that the place must be pretty poorly organized—and was that the kind of place you wanted to be treated in? I explained to her that while this duplication was certainly troublesome, it was a price you had to pay for the extra care that (theoretically) you got in a teaching hospital. "Besides," I said, "you should see the accounting department."

Alex accepted my explanation—sort of—but what really peeved her, beyond the mere repetition, was how she was personally treated in this process. Dr. Dolan, his CF clinic associates, and the Fitkin 5 nurses all dealt with Alex as a human being, but the teaching staff often acted as if Alex—or any patient—was simply some object, there to assist them on their way to hanging up a shingle so they could take Wednesday afternoons off and play golf.

Now, I don't think I'm being too critical. I think I appreciate the demands placed on doctors. For example, I don't think that a doctor is always obligated to take a great deal of time to explain to some child the procedures of a one-time operation; probably most kids don't want to know all that much anyway. However, for a child with a chronic illness, the situation is different—no matter how old the child. Tom Dolan recognized that. He appreciated that Alex, like a lot of CF children, understood her own pathology better than anyone else, better even than people who introduced themselves as "Doctor." Invariably, we knew when it was time for Alex to go back in the hospital, because she would signal us with transparent talk about how she sure hoped she didn't have to go back into the hospital anytime soon. She knew.

Unfortunately, the worst two episodes that Alex experienced with young doctors both came in the fall of 1979, when she was so sick that any sort of adversary treatment was simply cruel. The first took place one afternoon in October shortly after her lung collapsed when Tina Crawford happened to be visiting Alex. A particularly officious young doctor brought a bunch of students over to examine Alex. He pointed to the tube in her chest, explaining that the incision of an inch or so had been made while she was under a local anesthetic, and then he declared. "This procedure is not very painful to the patient." Immediately, he proceeded with his lecture.

All the years of hearing these cocky young experts talking at her as if she were a body on display, as if a child—a sick child—could not be a real person, welled up in Alex. "Wait!" she suddenly cried out.

But the doctor ignored her and kept right on with his spiel. "No, wait you," she said again, louder still, and tugging at his sleeve this time, too.

He stopped. He had to. Alex had made him stop. And, only then, with a condescending look of annoyance, he turned down to her. "Yes, what is it, dear?"

"How do you know?" Alex said.

"What, dear?"

"How . . . do . . . you . . . know?"

"I'm sorry, but—"

"Have you ever had a big tube stuck in you and then taken out again?"

"Well, no, I, I—"

"Then don't you tell me—or them—it doesn't hurt. Because I don't like being lied to."

Tina says some of the students snickered at the doctor, but he only mumbled an apology, laughed it off, and hurried out to find a more pliant child.

A much worse episode occurred the next month, the day after Thanksgiving. Alex had been back in the hospital for a couple of weeks and was anxiously looking forward to being released. But that morning her lung collapsed again—only nobody in authority would believe her. Nobody would listen to her. She was only a patient; only a child, dying.

Alex herself knew immediately that her lung had collapsed. After all, the memory of her previous collapse was clear enough—only six weeks past. But the young resident on the floor seemed threatened that an eight-year-old could be usurping his diagnostic responsibility. He told Alex she was wrong, her lung had not collapsed. Not only that, he refused to give her X rays. Fortunately, Carol, accompanied by her mother, arrived that morning for a visit. They listened to Alex and urged the doctor at least to call in Dr. Dolan. He lied to them and told them he had already notified Dr. Dolan, and he would be along in time. No layperson was going to tell him a thing.

The greatest irony is that when Alex had been released from the hospital the time before, Tom Dolan had carefully explained to Carol what the symptoms of a lung collapse were, so that, if Alex ever did have another, Carol would understand the problem and rush Alex to the hospital. That way she could, as much as possible, avoid great pain. And here Alex was actually *in* the hospital, in *her* hospital, describing exactly the symptoms Tom Dolan had explained to Carol, and still the know-it-all resident wouldn't listen to Alex and wouldn't listen to Carol.

It devastated Alex. She was so upset that later that afternoon—still before the resident would let her go for X rays—Alex called in Claudia Cameron, who helped run the play program in the ward, and dictated her account of the episode. Alex knew that what was happening was wrong, and she damn well wanted it on the record. Claudia took down what Alex told her:

"I started coughing *really, really* hard. Then it felt really hard to breathe. I started to cry. Wanda came in and I said, 'I think I have a collapsed lung.'

"Then I got up to go to the bathroom and I started to scream. Barbara came. 'My side hurts,' I said. I put on nasal prongs to give me oxygen and it made me feel a little better. Then Barbara said, 'What would you like best, besides your parents?' I said, 'I would like a nurse by me.' Maribeth stayed with me while Barbara checked IVs. It felt comfortable that the nurses were with me. Sue, Wanda, and Maribeth all took turns watching me. I fell asleep. In between my sleep I would cough.

"After a while my mother and Nana were here, and I started to cry because I was so happy they had come. I took another rest but I coughed some more. My mom started crying because she was unhappy for me."

That is how a child feels when she is sick and hurting and they don't trust her.

Finally, the obvious could no longer be contradicted, and the resident agreed to let Alex go for X rays. They revealed exactly what Alex had told everybody six hours before, that her lung had collapsed.

We were infuriated—all the more because Alex had suffered so needlessly—but the incident did recede rather quickly from her consciousness for the simple reason that the new collapse meant she would have to stay in the hospital longer. Soon, that meant much more to Alex than the suffering and indignity she had been forced to endure on that one day, November 23. She was beginning to think more and more about her death.

I sat down and wrote a long letter to the head of the department of pediatrics and to the chief of staff of the hospital. I began: "I don't want anybody's hide. I don't want anybody to eat crow." The damage was done to Alex, and to drag it out, to carry a grudge, would only create an atmosphere that, I was sure, would make it more uncomfortable for her in the hospital. But: attention must be paid. At least if I made known what had happened, then maybe it would be less likely to happen again. Maybe the next young man who wants to be a doctor will listen to a child. And so I outlined all the events, carefully, and then I concluded:

> In the days since, I must say that many people at the hospital have commiserated with us, saying, "Well, at least no harm was done." They have been well meaning, and I've appreciated their thoughtfulness, but I suppose it depends on what you mean by harm. I gather that in hospital talk "no harm done" is a polite euphemism for, "Look, it's okay, nobody died, did they?"
>
> But, for me, I think much harm is done when a little child, who suffers much too much and much too unfairly already, has to endure a great deal of extra pain that isn't necessary. I think harm is done when people like my wife and myself have been shown that

we better not trust a hospital we must depend upon. I think harm is done when a little girl who must spend part of her existence in a hospital ward finds out that the people who care for her have no faith in what she tells them—even have no faith in her pain. . . . So yes, harm was done, and I fear the most was done to Yale–New Haven Hospital . . .

Something is drastically wrong with the system, and I hope, by telling you all this, that the system will be corrected. I know you're a teaching hospital, but I hope it can also be taught that patients (even eight-year-olds) and their parents are not so many school supplies.

I got nice replies from the doctors, and recently I read that Yale–New Haven was voted one of the top ten hospitals in the United States. I have no doubt that is true. Yet I fear that everywhere too many young doctors will not listen to children. I don't think they teach that very well.

CHAPTER 22

As bad as that occasion was, there was to be an even more heartbreaking incident a few days later. How Alex survived this emotionally is still beyond me.

The tubes had come out of Alex's chest after another week or so, and she was finally scheduled to go home on December 3. Carol was at college that day, so I was going to pick Alex up around lunchtime and drive her back to Westport. The night before, when I had been up visiting, she had been especially excited. She even wanted to know if we could drop by her school for a few minutes as soon as we got home so she could say hi to everybody. As weak as she had grown, Alex was more stir crazy than ever before; she'd been in the hospital for about six of the last eight weeks, all under more confining conditions than she was used to; besides, she hurt and she didn't want to die in the hospital.

In midmorning, I got a call from Yale–New Haven. Alex's lung had gone again. I rushed up, and when I got to her room we only hugged and held each other. There was nothing to say. Finally, she pulled back and looked at me. I had never seen such utter despair upon her face. Finally, this is what she said: "Daddy, why does God hate me?"

• • •

Now that I was there, they were ready to make the chest incision and insert the tube. The first time Alex had a collapsed lung—a pneumothorax, it was called—she had been given a large dosage of painkiller, and it really knocked her out; she slept for hours and was groggy many more. Thereafter, even though she was so frightened of pain, she seemed all the more frightened that she might never wake up, and so she told the doctors only to give her a local.

We did not know it at the time, but this would be the last occasion when Alex would—could—have the tubes inserted. Carol and I, and Alex, feared that it would keep happening, again and again, the final cruel indignity, but what we did not know was that, after this time, Tom Dolan doubted that her body could stand the trauma of another cut. There was so little left of her.

And so I carried Alex into her treatment room. By then she had prepared herself fairly well, but as soon as she saw that stark table where she was to lie and receive her shot and her incision, she stiffened and was the little girl again. "No, not yet! Not yet!" she cried, and she clung to me as tight as ever she had.

I remember noticing that both nurses there turned away from us at that moment, because, for all they might see, day after day in a hospital, there was such an awful intimacy to Alex's gesture that they could not bear to intrude on us. I only held Alex and tried to comfort her more.

And, in time, when she had composed herself, she said, "All right. I'm ready now." And so she was.

So I started to lay her down where they would cut her open. And in that moment, I could not hold back any longer; one tear fell from all those welling in my eyes. And Alex saw it, saw my face as I bent to put her down. Softer, but urgently, she cried out, "Wait!" We all thought she was only delaying the operation again, but instead, so gently, so dearly, she reached up, and with an angel's touch, swept the tear from my face.

I will never know such sweetness again in all my life.

"Oh, my little Daddy, I'm so sorry," is what she said.

One nurse turned and bowed her head and began to sob. The other could not even stay in the room. She ran off to compose herself. It was some time before we could get going again.

First, they spread pumpkin-colored soap over where Alex was to be cut. I held her hand. Then they brought out the needle, a huge horse needle. I squeezed her hand, and she squeezed mine back, harder, harder, as they jammed it deeper into her. She cried. And then they started to cut her. Can you imagine what it is like to be with your child when they are cutting open her chest?

And all for nothing, too. I knew that. It wasn't really going to do any good. It wasn't going to save her. It might not even help her. All we knew for sure was that it would hurt her. But it had to be done. It had to be done, so I held my baby's hand, and the doctor cut through the orange goo as if she were a jack-o'-lantern being sliced up for Halloween, and then he brushed away the blood, stuck a tube in her, sat back and said, "Okay."

"It's over," I said.

Alex said, "Thank you, Daddy."

"Alex wasn't that specific about finding out what was happening to her until after the chest tubes," Barbara told me later. But at that point she seemed to grasp the utter hopelessness of her plight. And yet, how unfair it was—one more difference—that as she could not live life like the rest of us, neither could she even talk of death to those closest to her. You see, in many ways she felt she had to protect us—her little Daddy, her beloved mother and brother—more than we

163

her. There were a couple of occasions, after some new and horrible setback, when she directly advised Tom Dolan, "Now, don't tell my mother, because she worries so much."

One day Carol was with Alex, and a whole bunch of the other kids started coming into her room. She had the lung tube in her and she was especially immobile, so Nancy and Claudia from Child Life had let Alex have the record player in her room. She was playing one of her favorite records, the one Marlo Thomas did for kids. A book comes with the record so you can get all the words right. The other children started coming in and they all began singing—happily shout-singing, the way kids do—and all of a sudden Carol realized they were singing the best song on the record, "Free to Be . . . You and Me," and Carol couldn't take that. She remembered, "When they find a cure, I'll be free, like everyone else." And she had to bolt from the room, crying. Carol could stand anything but that: *free.*

Alex watched her go. Alex knew. Barbara recalls episodes when Carol was especially upset and morose that Alex would purposely act her worst, very fresh and bratty, to divert her mother's emotions—Carol would then grow annoyed at Alex, rather than sad. One time Barbara remembers that Carol was fixing Alex's hair, fighting to hold back the tears as she made her dying child pretty, and Alex suddenly started making such a nuisance of herself that Carol finally got so irritated she said, "Alex, if you don't stop acting like this, I'm going to leave this room."

And Alex immediately did one more exasperating thing, and left Carol with no alternative but to storm off to the canteen for a cup of coffee. As soon as she was gone, Barbara said, "Alex, that was horrible of you. You were really mean to your mother. You shouldn't be like that."

And Alex said, "Oh, Barbara, you don't understand. She was just being too sad, and that wasn't good for her. But if I told her I didn't want her around that would've hurt her. This was best for her. I'll be all right when she comes back."

Barbara shakes her head now, remembering Alex. "It's a horrible thing," she says, "but the death of a child in the hospital—any hospital—can become almost routine for the staff. That's even more the case with a cystic fibrosis child, because it happens regularly enough, and each death happens much the same way. We can see it coming. There've been several children I especially liked who got very sick, and as they came closer to dying, I always made myself hold back. But with Alex, she was so special, so caring of others, even when she knew she was dying, that you couldn't do that, you couldn't back away from her, because she just pulled it out of you."

Alex began to inquire more directly into the implications of the lung collapses. Where does this go? What does this mean? Why does my lung keep collapsing? Will it ever stop collapsing . . . so I can go home? She began to talk more and more to Tina about cystic fibrosis itself. "Tina," she said one day, "this disease has gotten so much *bigger* than me."

"Bigger?"

"Yeah, it's really in control of me. You know what I think?"

"No, what, Alex?"

"I think it's angry with me. Maybe I should try and be its friend."

"How?"

"Well, that's why I think I shouldn't take my medicines. You see, my medicines fight the germs and the cystic fibrosis. Maybe if I were its friend and I didn't fight back it wouldn't be so angry with me."

As childish as this sounds, it is, in fact, a form of denial often practiced by much older CF patients, who hate their disease so much that they begin to hate everything associated

165

with it, including their therapy. So they end up not doing therapy, because that is the only way they know of striking back at the disease itself.

But Alex never evaded the greater issue. "Will I die, Barbara?"

"Not right now. Why?"

"I'm afraid."

"What are you afraid of, Alex?"

"I'm afraid most that when I'm gone, my mommy and my daddy will be so sad. And I'm especially afraid about Chrish."

"Why?"

"Because then he'll be all alone. My mommy and my daddy have each other, but Chrish won't have any other brother or sister." More and more, Barbara said, Alex worried about her big brother, and how he would be alone.

One evening, near the end of her last stay in the hospital, I told Alex I had to go home for the night. I added, to assuage my guilt at leaving her, that I hadn't seen Chris all day and should spend some time with him, too. And she just shook her head and said, "Oh, Daddy, I'm breaking up the family, aren't I?"

"Of course not, Alex."

And then she began to look like she was going to start to cry. "Oh, Daddy, I want to come home so much. I've been up here so long I don't even remember what my little house looks like."

She was so scared then that she would never escape the hospital. Cyd remembers that, starting about that time, Alex would occasionally allay her nervousness by reverting to baby talk—something she hadn't done in years. I think she had a greater fear of dying in the hospital than she did of actually dying.

From then on, too, I started staying nights in the hospital. There was no longer a need to worry about setting a precedent. There weren't going to be many more nights. So either Carol or I slept in the room with Alex most every night the rest of the way. Alex never really wanted to be left alone anymore. She needed to know that someone she knew and loved would be there with her if she started to die. Apparently, most dying children eventually enter this phase. It is like being afraid of the dark; if you just have someone with you, then the dark is not frightening; it may even be more comforting than the light. Alex just didn't want to be alone.

Finally, too, Alex turned to Dr. Dolan for some official confirmation. "I'm not going to live much longer, am I?" she said, looking him square in the face. He hesitated. He had been through this sort of thing before with other dying children, and, anyway, he knew very well that he could not kid Alex. But he was trying to find just the right words. She grew impatient for his answer, and told him, "You have to tell me the truth, because I'll know if you're lying to me."

"Oh, I know you will, Alex," Dr. Dolan said. "I can't fool you."

"Well?"

"Well, Alex, I do think you'll go home, I do believe you'll get out of here . . . but no . . . no, I don't think things look too good for you."

And Alex smiled at that and reached out and patted Dr. Dolan's hand, to make it easier for him. "Okay," was all she said.

It was a couple days later, at her most philosophical, that Alex chose to first bring the subject up within the family. Thank God, it was with Carol. "Why me, Mother?" she said—but not a whining complaint, just the simple question. Alex was not saying why did it *have* to be me? She was only asking: Why do you *suppose* it was me?

I don't know how Carol did it. But she was prepared for the question, and she said, "Well, Alex, God must have a reason, and I think maybe that reason is because God knew that you would be the best at showing other people how to live and how to be brave."

Alex only nodded; that made sense to her.

I had to go out of town for a few days on December 11, so I went up to the hospital to spend an extra amount of time with Alex before I took off. Things were not going at all well. The tubes in her chest should have been registering minus five, whatever that means, but they were only down to minus one. I understood by now that any future operations could only be tried at the risk of her life. Yet there was no reason to believe that one of her lungs wouldn't collapse again. One way or another, it just didn't seem that she would ever leave the hospital alive.

And yet, there Alex was when I arrived, just beaming, her whole face painted like a clown. I mean a complete professional job, all white and red, bright and cheery, diamonds around her eyes, and, on her cheeks, those big red balls she herself used to put on the faces of all the people she drew. An expert in makeup had come by and painted the kids. We laughed and joked, Alex carried on like a clown, and we even talked about the circuses we should have gone to. Her spirits picked up even more later in the afternoon, because Mrs. Beasley, from the third grade, and another one of her favorite teachers at the school, Mrs. Sherwood, came by to visit her.

"Daddy," she said, as soon as they left, "do you think I can get back to school before Christmas?"

"If your lungs keep getting better, sure you can."

She shook her head with determination at that. "Oh, Daddy, now I'm sorry about those things I told you. I'm going to keep on hoping. I am! I promise you. You have to hope, don't you?"

"Yeah, I really think we all have to."

"Is hoping exactly like wishing?"

"Hmmm." I'd never thought about that one before. "Yeah, pretty much, I guess."

"I think hoping is more like, you know, you really can expect it. Really," Alex said. "I think wishing is more like dreams."

"That's an awfully good explanation."

"But neither one of them is like praying," Alex went on. She had thought a lot about this.

"No?"

"No, hoping and wishing are okay, because they don't involve God and Jesus the way praying does." That was the word she used: *involve.*

"I think that's absolutely right," I said, and just then Carol arrived, unexpectedly. Neither Alex nor I had anticipated her coming that evening, since I was going to spend the night. Alex was especially excited, because her mother would get to see her in her clown getup. She clapped her hands and cheered.

"Oh, it's Mommy," she cried. "Oh, Mother! My wish came true." And then she paused and looked over to me, her head tilted a little. "But not the real wish," she said. It was a small private joke of hers.

But, sure enough, some hopes are fulfilled. Even Alex caught a little good fortune now and then, and that time, for no real reason, the lungs held after the tubes were removed. She seemed to sense it. Carol and her mother came visiting one day, and they brought a tutu for Alex. It was just her meat: garish and shiny, with sparkles all over it, and she put it on and went down the hall of the ward, spinning around and laughing, sort of using her IV pole as a dance partner. "It was incredible," Carol told me later. "She was really carried away, and when the children and their parents and the nurses came out of the rooms, it gave her even more energy, and—you should have seen it—she really laid it on. The more the people would clap, the more elaborate her dancing would get—

and here she was, shackled to an IV pole the whole time. But it had all just sort of happened, it was spontaneous, and then Alex realized that this was it, this was her last dance performance before a crowd, and she would give them a great show. And that's what she did."

A few days after that Alex was released from Yale–New Haven Hospital for the last time. It was December 15, 1979, the day before my forty-first birthday.

"There's no more I can do for her," Tom Dolan told me. "She knows that, too. Some kids, when they sense that, give up on the doctor right away, but Alex hasn't. She's never blamed me for her disease. She's a wonderful child. I just pray for all of you that she lives some time past Christmas, because I've seen families where the child died over the holidays, and then, every Christmas after that was ruined for them."

Always before, when she left Fitkin 5, Alex would laugh and say something like this to Barbara: "Okay, I'll see you the next time they make me come back to the stupid old place." But this time, before Barbara knew what hit her, Alex said only, "Good-bye," and threw her arms around her. To Cyd, alone, the night before, in her room, Alex said, "Good-bye forever," and then, to a new nurse, one she liked but hadn't grown that close to, Alex was almost matter of fact. "I'm going home to die now," she said, "but don't you tell my Mommy or Daddy because it'll upset them."

Of course, Carol called me and told me that Alex was coming home, but Carol and Chris pretended that I hadn't been advised of the good news. So when I came back from my trip that evening Alex was hidden in a closet, and I made a big to-do of saying loudly, "Well, let me get a quick bite, and then I'll go up to the hospital to see Alex." And at that, of course, she popped out of the closet, cried out, "I love you," and hurried across the room to me, her arms flung open wide.

170

I can still visualize that so clearly, Alex running those few steps—running!—her face shining with joy, her laughter forming hope and wishes and prayer, all three, and I grabbed her and kissed her and held her as high as I could, as if she might really be a seagull drifting away, into the fog.

CHAPTER 23

Poor old Chaucer was growing more and more lethargic and aloof, and Chris had discovered a puppy down at the nearest pet store. It was a little white Lhasa apso, and he took Carol to inspect it while I was away. It was the cutest thing—a real puppy puppy, lively and bright eyed, floppy eared, love starved—and Chris told Alex all about it. The first thing Carol and Chris did for Alex when she got back from the hospital was to take her over to the store. Naturally, she fell in love with the little thing.

"What do you say?" Carol asked me. "It'll give Alex something to look forward to." Of course, I agreed.

Covering all bases, Alex wrote a special letter to Santa, too.

> Dear Santa Claus,
> I would like a little White furry Lapsa apso. I know I'm asking alot. But Santa it would make my life easier because of my disease. Santa I want this puppy more than anything in the world and thats the truth. Oh oh Santa this really really means a whole lot. And in fact it loves my mommy me my brother but it hasn't seen my father but I think he'd love

him. I hope I have convince you enough.
Love, Alex Deford

To be honest, I really don't think that Alex believed in Santa Claus anymore. On the other hand, I also don't think she saw any sense in getting deeply involved in that issue. I think, when you're a child dying, it is quite enough worrying about God and all that, without making too much of a fuss over Santa Claus. Besides, Alex knew this was going to be her last Christmas, so why not keep the string intact? She let herself go on believing.

Chris and I went down to the pet store and bought the little puppy, making arrangements to have it stay there until Christmas. Then, the last day before school let out for vacation, Carol took Alex over to school. She was so excited at that. It had been, after all, a wish. Not the real one, you understand, but a wish all the same. The whole Greens Farms Elementary School cheered Alex, and her own third-grade classmates surrounded her so that "we were squashing her," Aimee told me, and Mrs. Beasley had to cry out happily, "Come on now, back up from Alex. You don't want to hug all the health out of her." It was a happy, happy time, and Alex kept recounting those moments to me.

Of health, there was precious little left. Her face was drawn and pale, dominated by the blackness of her mouth and her eyes. Carol said to me, "It almost seems now as if her whole face is eyes." Alex had to sleep much of the time, and though once she had fought not to have to wear her nose prongs, now she welcomed them for the additional oxygen and comfort they brought her. Increasingly, she had to sleep in what almost amounted to a sitting position, propped up on piles of pillows, leaning forward on Tink, her big cuddly round lamb. Apparently, this posture helped open up her chest for an iota more of air. "You see, Daddy, when you have CF you must sit up like this or you get all scrooged up," Alex

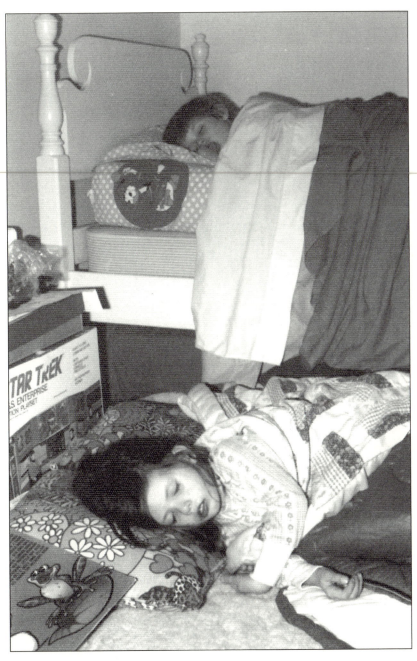

I'm not sure why Alex is sleeping on the floor on this occasion, with Chris above in his bed. Alex is four years old here, January 1976.

explained to me patiently, as if she were telling me how to play a game or put on a boot.

As always, Chris would start off the night sleeping next to her, but from then on, alternately, Carol or I would come in, move Chris back to his bed, and take his place next to Alex. Her breathing was so labored that it was actually difficult for me to sleep with all the commotion, and, listening, I was sure that it must hurt her just to breathe. Her knees were all swollen up from her "just arthritis," and when I rubbed her back, her spine jutted out so that it seemed as if the bones must soon break through the skin. Her liver condition had worsened, and God only knows what else. This cursed disease. This evil monster. Not even Alex worried anymore about her fingers.

The worst was when suddenly Alex couldn't get any air at all, and she would shoot up in bed, crying, "Help me! Help me!" And it was all the more horrible that there wasn't really anything we could do when that happened. Mostly we would just run to her and console her.

"What can I do, darling?"

"Just hold me tight when I finish coughing."

Often, then, I would have to leave the house, go out in the cold to find some fresh air for myself. Two or three times I even went down to the beach on Long Island Sound and walked—the wind blowing cold life back into my face. God forgive me that I had to get away. *Help me! Help me!* Again and again; I shall hear my child call out for as long as I live. Once, weeks after Alex was dead, Carol, hearing a sound, suddenly started to run up the stairs, reflexively, to Alex's room. *Help me! Help me! Just hold me tight when I finish coughing.*

It was four days before Christmas when Carol said, "I think we better bring that puppy home today."

At first, I didn't want to. I wanted to think that at least we could make every effort to have a Christmas as typical as

176

possible, and, also, I thought of all those awful newspaper Wirephotos I had seen through the years, of Christmas trees set up in August and September for some child who would not live till Christmas. "Let's wait, please," I said. But when I slept with Alex that night, it was an even more frightening experience, and so, when I got up the next morning, first thing, I wrote her a note from Santa, explaining that the puppy was getting so lonely at the North Pole that he and Mrs. Claus and the elves and the reindeer—everybody—had discussed it, and they thought it would be a good idea to bring him down to Westport a few days early so that he could be with an especially good little girl.

It was all worth it. We named the little thing Buffalo, and even when we put him on her lap, and he rolled around and nipped at her and made her cough from all the action, it seemed a fair price to pay. On Christmas Eve, Alex said she thought she ought to write Santa a thank-you note when he came back with the regular Christmas bounty. She left it down by the tree. It said: "Dear Santa, Thank you for the puppy. Here's some milk and cookies for you. Love, Alex xoxoxxxxxoooxxxxx." Alex usually wrote at greater length. Then I noticed these initials down at the bottom of the letter: "AD:cmd." Chris had written the note for her. She had grown too weak even to write out a few lines.

Christmas, of course, was especially hard. On the night of the twenty-third some carolers came by. Prominent among them was Joan McFarland, a professional singer Alex knew and adored, and she was absolutely thrilled that a real pro had come to her house. Sure, it wasn't Bobby Vinton, but it was a terrific Christmas present. I held Alex up to the window at the front door, and she was so transfixed by Joan and the other carolers that she didn't notice my crying. Oh, she probably did. But she didn't say anything. It was such a lovely scene, classic Christmas, the carolers bundled up against the cold, carrying candles, singing hymns. Carol and Chris stood at either side of me, and I held Alex in my arms. A year from this night, Carol and Chris and I would be on Waikiki, hearing the band from the Royal Hawaiian Hotel playing carols that drifted in the warm night across the sands.

But that was a long time away. Alex went to bed, happily exhausted, soon after the carolers left, and the next day was Christmas Eve, 1979. It rained. We came very close to a perfect white Christmas, but it was to be one of those peculiar winters when the temperature always got just over freezing so it rained every time it was supposed to snow.

In the afternoon we went to the children's carol service at our church, Christ and Holy Trinity. Alex had a new dress to wear: a bright red skirt, with a white blouse and a red string tie. It was very fancy, very feminine, and she adored it. Carol had also bought her a brand new pair of patent leather shoes. Christmas Eve was one of the few times Alex wore those shoes, and she had to be carried so much, even when she had shoes on, that when we went in to see her at the funeral home for the last time, before we closed the coffin up, I noticed that the shoes were hardly scuffed on the soles.

Alex got very tired during the carol service, but she came to life again for her favorite part. There was a crèche up by the altar, and every year Bruce Shipman, the assistant pastor, would call children up from the congregation, one by one, to put the Christmas figurines in place—starting with the bit players, the donkeys and shepherds, then moving on up to the stars. Alex had been especially delighted the Christmas before when Father Shipman had chosen her to put Mary in the crèche.

So when Father Shipman called for volunteers, Alex whispered to me, "I'm not going to raise my hand, Daddy. I've missed so many Sunday schools in the hospital that it wouldn't be fair." I didn't press the point, and we sat quietly and watched other children waving their hands and marching up. But at last, when it came to the final figurine, the Angel—

after Baby Jesus Himself—Father Shipman ignored all the remaining petitioners, pointed to Alex, and called out her name.

Whatever reservations she may originally have had about playing a part in the ceremony vanished. She beamed, popped right up, marched smartly to the crèche, took the Angel from Father Shipman, and put it in its assigned place, looking down on the whole scene. Of course, as she came back to her seat, all I could think was that the next time Alex came down the aisle of this church, it would be in a box.

She explained things to me when she got back to her seat. "It's sort of like a guardian angel, Daddy," she said. "I thought it was okay for me to do the guardian angel, don't you?"

"Oh, absolutely."

We played more carols on the stereo when we got home, but Alex was so tired from church that it was no trick getting her to go to bed early. She did express some concern that her dear old pal, Chaucer, might have had his feelings hurt, what with Buffalo being brought in to share his turf, but I assured her that Santa would certainly bring something extra nice for Chaucer this Christmas—a dog stocking or something like that—and that soothed her. "Daddy," she said, "everybody should have a nice Christmas, even dogs," and when she went through her usual prayer routine, she made sure to ad lib special supplications for all the children in the poor countries, that they would have a Christmas as nice as hers, here in the United States. Then, propped up on her pillows, quickly she fell off to sleep.

Merry Christmas, 1979! We opened all our stockings together in Carol's and my bed, and afterward I stumbled downstairs, barely able to see through my tears, to light the tree. All I kept thinking was that this would be the last Christmas that I would ever have Santa Claus in my house, and this would be the last Christmas that I would ever have a daughter. It was, of course, perfectly foolish and masochistic to go around—to go out of my way—thinking things like that, but that was how I was. I couldn't help myself, and now I'm not sorry. I think Alex is more vivid to me because I punished myself with her every last this and her every last that.

The Christmas itself, the opening of presents, was sort of a letdown, though. Carol and I had gone out of our way to make this an extra-special, expensive Christmas. Chris got a neat, grown-up bike, Chaucer got his stocking full of dog goodies, and we gave each other some nice clothes. But all we really wanted was to have Alex with us—the rest was altogether superfluous. We were living out those classic Christmas stories—like *The Gift of the Magi*—that celebrate the message being more important than the presents. Only, of course, those stories always have happy endings.

Alex herself had specifically requested a microscope (along with the usual array of pretty clothes and accessories, dolls, and jewelry). I have no idea whatsoever why she wanted a microscope—it was hardly her kind of thing—but that was her heart's desire, and so, naturally, we got her a microscope. That Christmas, if Alex had asked for hand grenades and poisonous snakes, we would have gotten her the finest hand grenades and poisonous snakes available.

We had a nice morning together, and by the time all the presents were open, Alex was so exhausted that she didn't even bother to go up to her room. She was still in her quilted blue robe, and she just lay down on the sofa in the living room, and dropped off immediately, snuggled up with Tink.

We all looked at her there. How beautiful she still managed to be, even as the disease had ravaged her, even as she breathed in agony. I took movies of her just lying there.

When Alex woke up she found Carol in another room. Christmas afternoon is always a most peaceful time, unless somebody has been fool enough to give a child a drum or turn

Alex and her friend Jonah play grown-ups with Jonah's baby brother, Jake. This was sometime near the end.

on a football game. Carol was just sitting there reading when Alex came to her. "Mother," she said, "it's been a wonderful Christmas for me. I got everything I wanted."

Carol kissed Alex and hugged her and told her how happy she was to hear that. But then, suddenly, Alex stamped her foot. "Oh, why did I have to get this disease? I hate it. It's so unfair." And she started to cry a little. But then she caught herself again. "But having Buffalo will make things different. He will. He was a wonderful present."

181

"I'm so glad, darling."

"But, of course, you know what would have been the best present of all." Carol nodded. Alex said it anyway, "A cure for my disease." Carol nodded again. There wasn't anything she could say, and she could tell that Alex wanted to say something more, anyway. And she did. She said, "You know, Mother, you know what I've wondered about a lot?"

"No, what's that?"

"Just what it's like not to have a disease. I've often thought about that, Mother. Just what it would be like not to have a disease. I wouldn't even ask for forever. Just for a day I'd like to wake up one morning, and not have any pain or be sick or anything. Just once to be free."

Merry Christmas.

CHAPTER 24

Something changed once Alex made Christmas. We all relaxed a bit. There was more pain for her, poor thing, but there was a certain peace, too. The battle was o'er. In fact, when I slept with Alex on Christmas night, there were a couple of times when she was suddenly still and quiet with her breathing, and I thought she must have died right then. And I could have accepted it, too.

But she was not quite ready to go. After the silence, both times, she suddenly started coughing, and crying, "Help me! Help me!" And then, when she was better, "I'm sorry I had to wake you, Daddy."

The next night, when Carol slept with Alex, she had the exact sensation I had, and twice she came in to wake me and tell me that she thought Alex was going. I told her I had had the same fears the night before, but I went into Alex's room, trying to act causal, as if I regularly dropped by at two in the morning. "Don't worry, Daddy," Alex said right away.

"Oh, I'm not worried," I said. "I was just wondering how you were sleeping."

"Fine," Alex said, and brightly, too. "You know, I'm just waking up and coughing a lot." That's all; everything's relative. We had all misplaced so much reality by then.

But nothing could calm Carol for long, and when she came for me again, in even more desperate fear, I moved into Alex's room and climbed in with my two girls. When Alex was through coughing again and had caught her breath as best she could, she spoke up, rather conversationally. "You know," she said, "that dog has just changed my life so much."

"How's that, Princess?"

"Can't you tell, Daddy? Now I don't talk about my disease that much."

I wanted to laugh at the madness of it all.

And so Alex lived some more. She lived to see the New Year, A.D. 1980. I saw it clearly in my mind for the first time: ALEXANDRA MILLER DEFORD, 1971–1980. We woke up both Alex and Chris at a quarter to twelve, and watched the ball fall in Times Square at midnight. Nineteen-eighty. She'll never make a census, I thought. Isn't that funny? Alex was born a year after the last one, and they wouldn't count again till April, when she'd be gone. She'll never be counted. That seemed wrong, somehow. Happy New Year.

The holidays were gone for good, officially, and that did make life more normal. I took a couple brief business trips down to Virginia during the following two weeks, a fact that frightens me horribly now when I think back on it—that I might have been away from Alex when she died— but at the time she seemed to have achieved a certain equilibrium, and once we were past the holidays we seemed to convince ourselves that death was, somehow, no longer imminent. Besides, I was trying to occupy myself some in order to—let's face it—escape. I was always more of a coward than Carol.

Tina Crawford was a godsend. She spent more and more time with Alex those last days, spelling Carol when I was away. Tina has reassured me some, too. "Don't worry," she says, "Alex never would have died without you. I know it sounds crazy, but children pick their time to die."

Tina was wonderful in many ways, not the least that she was someone outside the family in whom Alex could confide. To the end, Alex protected her family, preferring to maintain a certain comforting fiction with us. Tina gave her the outlet she needed.

One night Tina volunteered to baby-sit for us, so that I could get Carol out of the house, if only for a few hours. When Tina tucked Alex in, she asked her if she wanted to read or play a game, or maybe just snuggle and chat. Alex opted for the latter, and they lay there for a while, Alex leaning forward on Tink, trying to breathe better. By then, understand, a great deal of her life was devoted merely to the supposedly simple business of breathing.

A few moments passed in dreamy silence, and then Alex heaved a sigh. Tina asked her what was up. "Oh, you know, Tina. I just keep getting weaker. I can't even sit through a game anymore. Nothing is getting better. It's hard when nothing ever gets better."

"I know."

"All I can do is think about things I used to do. Like when I could dance and play with my friends."

"Well, you do have a lot of nice things to think about," Tina said.

"When I was little, I was chubbier. I really was. I was healthy looking. But now, as I get older, I just get skinnier. You know what I think, Tina?"

"What?"

"Sometimes I think soon there'll be nothing left of me, nothing at all, and then I'll just float away." She let her hand drift up. Somewhere in the back of her mind Alex must have retained that imagery of the seagulls flying off into the fog in Maine.

"Float away?" Tina asked.

"Yeah, like a leaf in the wind, or maybe a balloon— *phfff*. Maybe I'll just float off like a balloon. Just like that." And Alex sighed again. "You know what's so scary?"

185

"No, what?"

"When I can't breathe, Tina. When I just can't breathe at all. I'm sorry, but I get all upset then, because I'm afraid I'll die and then I won't see my parents or Chrish again. And you know what else is scary, Tina?"

"What's that?"

"Some people die a very painful death. They do."

"Yeah, I know, Alex, but many more people die a peaceful death, because the doctors can give them special medicines to make it easy."

"Oh, yeah? I wasn't sure about that." And Alex relaxed a little then. This was obviously something reassuring, something she had wanted to know. Why couldn't I have figured that out? But then, even if I had, how could I have gone up to my dying child and talked to her about ways of dying? So it was especially good that Tina could tell Alex these things. And Alex rested on Tink, soothed some, it seemed. But suddenly she raised her head up and glanced around the room. "Look, Tina," she said.

"Look at what?"

"Just look all around, all around my room. Look at all the nice things I have. I have so many nice things, Tina. And I have a wonderful mother and a wonderful father and a wonderful brother and I have this new puppy now, and I live in this country, and I have so many friends, too. Isn't it funny? I have so much. But the only thing I've had bad luck in is my health." And she was quiet again, thinking. The room was soft in the half-light, still and quiet.

After a while, Tina said, "Alex, you were talking about people dying. What does that mean?"

"Well, it means a soul floating away to Heaven."

"Okay, what's a soul?"

"Gee, I kind of forget. What is it, Tina?"

"Well, people have different ideas about this, but I believe that a soul is all the beautiful things about a person, and

186

it lives in a peaceful place called Heaven. And it doesn't have any aches or pains."

Alex sat up all the way. "Not any? Not any *at all*?"

"That's right—none at all. And the soul also becomes part of everyone who ever knew that person, so they can't ever be away and miss each other too terribly."

"You know what?" Alex said then.

"What?"

"Angels live in Heaven, too."

"Sure," Tina said, "I knew that. Why, there're even some angels who wear tutus." Alex let out a giggle. "No, I'm not kidding. They wear tutus, with shiny sequins all over them." And Alex really laughed at that, although being careful not to laugh too much and end up with a coughing fit.

"Here, touch," Tina said then, changing the subject. She was five months pregnant, and she took Alex's hand and placed it on her stomach. Alex felt the baby move and giggled again.

"Oh, I hope when this baby's born, it's a girl," she said, anxiously, curiously, but very definitely in a tone that acknowledged that she would never see the baby when it was born.

"I hope so, too," Tina said. She already had two boys—Jonah, Alex's classmate and good friend, and little Jacob, whom Alex had so loved to hold when she had been strong enough.

"What are you going to call it, Tina? I mean, if it's a girl?"

"Well, maybe Zoe—" Right away, Alex made a face. "You don't like Zoe? Go on now, Alex, tell me the truth."

"No, not really, Tina. I'm sorry."

"That's okay. So, how do you like Jennifer? Or Kate?"

"Oh yeah," Alex said, brightening.

"Either one?" Alex nodded. "Well then, I'll name her Jennifer or Kate."

"That's nice," Alex said.

"And I've got a middle name all picked out, too," Tina said.

"What's that?"

"Alex," Tina said. "Whatever her first name will be, her middle name will be Alex," and she took Alex's hand and laid it back upon her child in her belly.

There was so little of anything that Alex could do any longer. Her friends remember little Buffalo yanking playfully at her braids, but she was too weak even to shoo him away. The last time she ever went out on her own, when I left her over at Aimee's a week before she died, Alex could hardly walk, and much less dance, and so she asked Aimee to dance for her. "Alex just got so slow," Wendy says. "I was going to color with her one day in her room, and she said, 'No, Wendy, I'll just rest now and watch you color.'"

Carol tried to take her out to lunch every day. They would pick different restaurants—Burger King, Friendly, the McDonald's way down in Norwalk—and when they would drive home they would sing together. It just started up naturally, and then it became an instant custom, the two of them singing at the top of their lungs in the car as they drove along. "You Are My Sunshine" was the favorite. Whatever else they sang, they did that one every day for sure.

But every day it grew more difficult. Alex was breathing so loudly, with such difficulty, that everybody in the restaurants stared at her, and Carol knew that was hurting her, even if they both pretended it wasn't going on. More important, Alex just didn't like to be away from her oxygen that long anymore. So one day—Carol was pretty sure it would be the last time they could go out together—after they had lunch, they also went to a little shop, called Sweet Pea, which has lots of stuffed animals and cute handmade toys. Carol carried her all around the shop. Alex had to be carried most everywhere now.

Then they drove home, singing "You Are My Sunshine" as loud as they could. There was a lot of laughing, even though Alex surely understood, too, that soon she wouldn't even be able to do a simple thing like that anymore. Down the street from our home, there was a big old house that was being done over. January, with the trees bare, and no curtains up yet, you could look right in from the road and see how they were fixing it up inside. The days before Carol and Alex had both spotted a fancy ceiling fan with all sorts of lights and everything. And this time, as they went by the house, Alex said, "You know, Mother, I wish I had the money to buy you and Daddy something really nice. I'd like to buy you a fan like that, because I want you to have something nice to remember me with."

After that Alex seldom even left her bedroom, and she kept the oxygen on almost all the time. She could still laugh at Benny Hill, though, still chuckle over whatever jokes Chris brought back from his school, still see the humor all around her. One day Tina brought Jonah over after school to visit, and he climbed into bed with her, and together they read Alex's favorite book of poems, *Where the Sidewalk Ends,* by Shel Silverstein. At one point, Alex started laughing so hard at a poem that both Carol and Tina began to cry—the incongruity of it all. It was almost as if she were literally going to die laughing.

A few days later, when Jonah heard that Alex had died, he went up to his room and wrote this.

I still think that you can hear Alex'es
laugh. I always Like when she laughed. I felt
like I would laugh along. I feel and ecpect her
to just walk in my room and sit down and then
I feel said when she doesent come in. If only

189

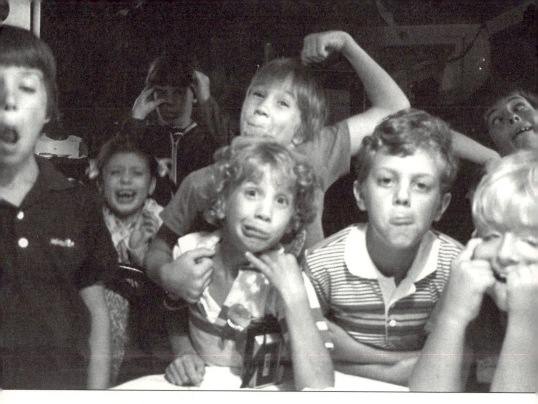

I believe this was a birthday party for Jonah Crawford. Anyway, that's Alex breaking up in the background, middle left.

time could stop when she was alive. She would still be here. She used to call me up all the time and Pretend to be Other people but her hestairical laugh gave it away. It made me happy that I knew her but its sad that shes not alive any more.

On that Thursday, the seventeenth, I came back from Virginia—"Oh, my little Daddy is back," she cried—and later that day, my brother Gill, who had found an excuse to come East from Los Angeles on business, traveled up to Connecticut to see Alex. She adored Gill and posed for her last pictures with him on Friday, sitting up in her bed, without her nose prongs, in her nightgown. She wore a pendant round her neck—always some jewelry—and Carol had also fixed her hair all up. She gave Alex a dry shampoo, and then she asked her

The last photo ever taken of Alex, a couple of days before she died, with her uncle, my brother Gill.

how she wanted her hair to be arranged. Alex said, "You do it the way you want to see me, Mother," and so Carol braided her hair with blue and white ribbons, and tied them up in loops with flashier big green ribbons. But pretty as that might have been, Alex had grown so extraordinarily gaunt that the ribbons seemed just to decorate each other. Only the smile was still her own. The rest of her had already been cut out for the stars.

Secretly, Alex showed Gill the Valentine she had made for Carol and myself. It was red and orange and pink, with several stick-ons of rainbows and hearts and kisses and teddy bears and lace doilies, and it read: "Mom & Dad are very special. There when I need them. They are loveing & gentle and as close as Tink. I love them more."

191

Friday afternoon I put Gill on the train to Boston, and I also finished making plans with one of Carol's friends for her to take Carol away on a little trip the next weekend. It didn't matter where they went. I just knew that Carol had to get away. Besides, as we both knew for certain, it would be no problem because Alex was going to live for at least a couple weeks more. We were both convinced of that.

We got a chance to get out that evening, too. Tina, dear Tina, came over to baby-sit with Alex. We had subscription theater tickets in New Haven. Chris spent the night out down the street at his friend Dmitri's house.

We came back around eleven, and after Tina left, that was when we sat downstairs and started chatting about the general situation. We agreed Alex had two weeks left, and then I said that I would have a long talk with Chris on Sunday, two days later. That seemed like a good time; it wouldn't be a school day. And it was at that moment when Alex called out, "Help me! Help me!"

It took us only a few moments to comprehend the truth. Gill was gone, Tina was back home, Christmas was well behind us, the Valentines were finished, and we had been able to enjoy a nice evening out. It was as good a time as any. It was now just past midnight, the beginning of January 19, and, I guess, as Tina had said, as much as a child could control these things, it was the best time for Alex to die, to find out after eight years what it was to be free.

CHAPTER 25

It was my night to sleep in with Alex, but Carol suggested that all three of us stay in her bed. Alex loved that idea, and we all piled in together. She would have liked to have been in the middle, between her mother and father, but that wasn't possible, because she had to keep her nose prongs on all the time, and they were attached, on a fairly short tube, to the oxygen compressor that was placed next to her side of the bed. The compressor made a horrible kind of wheezing sound, and it would kick out a thud at regular intervals. I hated that damn thing even as I had come to accept it as a part of Alex's room, her life, our house, our lives.

By that time the compressor didn't even bother me when I slept in with Alex, but this night, of course, none of us slept much at all. The pain was worse for Alex, and the pills we gave her seemed of little value. "Help me! Help me!" she would cry, more and more. Finally, around three-thirty, we called up Neil Lebhar, who was her pediatrician in town, and he came right over and gave Alex a shot of morphine. She was still alert enough to worry that the shot would hurt her, but the blessed thing took effect quickly and put her right out. Peace for her, thank God.

I went back into our bedroom then, so that we all might be more comfortable and get some sleep, and, in fact, it was past seven before I woke. I went downstairs to feed the dogs, and there, glancing out a window—I shall never forget this sight—there on the lawn, closer to the house than ever I had seen one, was a huge, coal-black raven, the bird of death. I am not being dramatic. It was there. Out loud, to myself, I said, "So this is what the day your child dies looks like." It was only a normal sort of January day, crisp and clear, the ground brown and ugly without any snow cover.

Carol and I had decided against calling Chris back home during the night—so long as we felt that we absolutely didn't have to—but now, around eight, Alex began stirring, and we phoned Dmitri's house and asked that Chris be brought back right away. He still wasn't certain what the full situation was, though. "Do we have to take Alex back to the hospital, Daddy?" he asked me when he came back into the house.

I only shook my head. "No, it's more than that."

"What is it?"

"Christian, I'm afraid Alex is going to die sometime today."

He shook his head at me in disbelief, and then fell into my arms and cried. Till then, he told me much later, he had never permitted himself to believe that this would ever really happen. And I had never had the courage or the chance to prepare him. I was going to go over all of it with him on Sunday, but here Alex was, dying on Saturday.

When he was better, I said, "Come on now, Alex wants to see you."

"Daddy, what do I say to her?"

"You don't have to talk about it. I know it's hard, but just be as casual as you can, and be as loving as you can."

"Does she know, Daddy?"

"I'm sure she does."

How she rejoiced when he came to her. "Oh, Chrish, my little brother, Chrish!" They chatted a while, and then

Alex saw how hard it was for him, and she suggested that he go play around. She was right. I don't think it would have been good for a ten-year-old boy to have to endure staying hours in his dying sister's room. Carol and I just told him to play nearby, keep us posted, and come back every hour or so to see his sister. It was better that way for Alex, too. It gave her a real treat whenever he popped back in. Somehow it even made things seem a little normal when Chris would come in and tell her all the mundane little boyish things he'd been doing outside or over at Dmitri's for the past hour or so.

Alex would doze off now and then, and that one time, midway through the morning, she asked me to go out and get her the root beer. By the time I got back to the house from the store she had drifted off again. I called our minister, Father Kennedy. I walked around. I tried to read the newspaper. The next day was the Super Bowl, Pittsburgh and somebody. At one point I walked over and looked behind the oxygen compressor, that huge awful box going wheeze, wheeze, thump, wheeze. There was an hour tabulator in the back, sort of a time odometer, which registered how many hours the machine had been on. You were billed by the hour. I had to fill out a form and mail it in every month—1186.5 hours, 1238.2 hours, or whatever. When I looked, the total read 1306 and something.

Right away it came to me: thirteens. Double thirteens are coming. The raven, now this. Alex will die when this machine reaches 1313 hours. I calculated that to be around two-thirty in the afternoon.

Both our ministers came. Father Kennedy was heading out of town for the day, but he dropped in and spoke to Alex and said a prayer. Later, Father Shipman, the assistant pastor, came by. He arrived about half-past twelve, and although Alex had declined markedly, she managed to ask Father Shipman a question. "Do you have to die to see God?" she said.

I don't think he was quite prepared for that. I know I wasn't. But he gathered himself and said, no, you didn't have to die to see God, because you could see Him all around, in all that He had created in this world—the birds and the animals and the trees and the flowers, everything.

Alex thanked him, and I could even see her smile at the thought of all those pretty things she loved. It was a good answer. On the other hand, after Father Shipman left, I got to thinking that it really wasn't fair for a child who was dying only to hear about God in terms of the things that living people see. So I reopened the subject, and I said that although none of us—not even a minister, not even Father Shipman— knows exactly what God in His Heaven looks like, it is unquestionably a much more beautiful place than earth. I said this was one of the advantages of dying.

"I don't want to die today," Alex said then. She wasn't being difficult. She knew she was going to die. She just said she didn't want to die *today.*

Carol said, "You know, Alex, when you die, you can see God and talk to Him and tell Him all about us. And we'll always be together, all four of us, because you'll keep an eye on us, and then we'll meet again in Heaven."

Alex took that all in, turning it over in her mind. She understood perfectly, but still, right to the last I suppose, she didn't want to absolutely, completely admit the whole truth. She would die with one wish—*the real one*—outstanding.

And then, as the day wore on, as the last of her life got away from her, Alex spoke less and less of anything. She was often uncomfortable and occasionally there were moments of unbearable agony, but they were brief, thank God, and never again did she suffer sustained periods of great pain, as she had the night before. Still, increasingly, it was difficult for her to make the effort to talk, and so mostly she only listened.

Carol took charge. She began to review Alex's life. I joined in. We never orchestrated this; we never plotted it. It just came naturally. After that we only really talked with Alex of two things: her life, and what we could guess of death. It didn't seem to be the time for small talk, when your child was dying.

So we brought up as many people as Alex knew and loved that we could recall. We talked of the things she had done with them, and of the joys she had given them, and they her. We talked of all the places she had been and of all the wonderful things we had done together. We talked about her school and about her room and her house and Chaucer and Buffalo and we even talked about the hospital and all her friends there. We talked about all the things Alex liked. What was her favorite song of all? She gave that some serious consideration and finally decided that it was "I Don't Wanna Play House," by Tammy Wynette. I went downstairs and found it and put it on her record player. Then we talked about the Broadway shows she had seen, and Benny Hill, who made her laugh, and all the dancing that she loved. Well, what we talked about was love. Love, love, love, Alex. We kept saying it.

And then we talked some about Heaven, too, about God and souls and angels. Carol told Alex that angels didn't have cystic fibrosis, they didn't even have touches of arthritis, so they could dance and play among the clouds in Heaven, all day, every day, and Alex smiled and managed to say yes, she already knew that, that she even had it on good authority that some angels wore tutus.

"Tutus!" said Carol. "Why, some angels wear tutus just like that shiny one you have with all the sequins."

"Really?" Alex managed to say.

"Oh yeah. Angels can get whatever kinds of tutus they want."

Alex nodded and smiled. "Mother?" she said.

"Yes?"

"What about wings?"

"Well, all angels have wings."

"I mean, will I get mine right away?"

"The first day," Carol said. "And then you can always be our guardian angel and watch over us."

And once more Alex smiled at us. But soon, again, those bursts of pain in her chest began to strike her, and she rose up from where she lay, her head on Tink, crying out to us. So often we had heard this, but now it seemed even more anguished, more shrill, perhaps, I suppose, because Alex was afraid that this time the pain would also include death in the bad bargain.

But each time the pain would subside, the great pain, and she would lie forward, where she was most comfortable, her head upon my chest. And one time, a little after one o'clock, when Alex leaned on me, she said, "Which way do I go?"— meaning, what's the best way for me to place my head? But it tore me up, the unintentional imagery. Such an ironic thing for someone to say in the face of death: *Which way do I go?*

And I chose to take the more obtuse meaning, and replied that way, "Any way you and God think is best, Alex."

She went along. "And Jesus, too, Daddy?"

"Oh yeah, Him, too. The three of you guys."

She smiled. But not long after that Alex became almost completely passive. That was the only way for her to go. When her brother came by again to see her around two o'clock, she forced her eyes open as soon as she heard him coming up the stairs, and that was when she said, for the last time, "I love you, Chrish."

That slight effort, to turn and speak, cost her so much, though, that when, shortly afterward, she wanted another sip of root beer, she could ask for it only by turning her head toward the glass and signaling for it with her eyes. Carol held the straw to her lips, and Alex managed a sip. And for thanks, one more smile. That was her last smile. She wasn't ever able again to muster a smile. Finally, the cystic fibrosis had even taken the smiles out of Alex. It was that mad at her.

Every conceivable effort had to be given over to breathing. She was so worn down, poor thing. Carol and I held her, first the one of us, then the other. We kept telling Alex about love. That constituted the conversation.

About twenty past two the hour counter on the back of the oxygen compressor turned to 1313. About a half-hour later Alex suddenly shot up. There was no cry this time, no energy left for that, but instead, there was upon her little face such a shocked expression, her eyes so full and wide, that both Carol and I were sure that this must be the end.

I believe it was meant to be, too. But something held Alex with us for just a little more. She had never wanted to be left out of anything, and yet she was robbed of so much of life, so I think she was at least determined, as much as was possible, to see what it would be like when she died. She found out it was like this: She fell onto my chest, and Carol clutched her hands and told her how much we loved her and always would. *So that is how I die: in my father's arms, my mother holding my hands. That is how.* So Alex knew now. In time she lay back on Tink.

She just lay there, and I reached under her gown and rubbed her back. Oh, God, the backbone stuck out so. Skin and bones. That was all that cystic fibrosis had left of her now. We talked more of love. That constituted the conversation, love.

A few minutes passed. There was nothing Carol and I could tell each other, even with our eyes. We were quiet now. Suddenly, Alex bolted up again. I would have known, without any doubt, that this was death, in all its power, but there had been the false alarm shortly before. Alex fell forward on my chest, her little body tumbling over my right leg that was crooked up on the bed. Carol took her hands once again, and, exactly as before, she told her how much we loved her and what a wonderful person she was.

And this time Alex raised up and away from me, but slowly, with purpose, not jerked by any pain or any forces but

199

her own, until she was almost fully sitting up, somehow supporting herself, and she looked directly at us, her eyes shifting from her mother to her father, so that both of us felt them boring into us.

I'm sorry, but this is how a child dies.

I can see those eyes, this moment, still. I see them constantly. But I could never describe them properly for what they meant, what they told. They were just absolutely wide open, so that even in death a little light could come in, and what they seemed to say was: *Can you believe it, Daddy? Can you believe it, Mother? It's really happening. Right now. Right now, I die.*

Oh, and how they also seemed to call to us with such unbelievable love.

And, at that, still just as open, they were also blank. The life had floated away, free. Alex's body stayed up for an instant or two more, but she was already up there with God. Imagine being eight years old and dead.

And then her little body, the skin and bones, tumbled over onto my right leg, and all this vile mucus, all this yukky that had hurt her and killed her, over all her years, all that began to ooze out of her mouth onto me. Oh, I was so glad. Even if it was too late to matter, I wanted that evil poison out of her. "Oh, Carol, she's died, thank God," I said.

Carol said, "Remember, she may still be here in this room. She may still hear us."

And so we both said, *"I love you, Alex,"* louder and louder, over and over, so that even if angels chattered she could not help but hear us over them.

Gently, then I laid Alex down by her Tink, not on him, as she had come to use him in pain, but next to him, as a child should be with her favorite toy animal. Carol drew her eyes shut and cleaned her off. Most all of the yukky had poured on me, so I took off my turtleneck, took off my pants, and there, in my underpants and socks, I got down on my knees by the bed where Alex had just died, and I thanked God for taking her out of the pain she had always known, till now.

I put on some new clothes while Carol tended to our little child. Alex looked so comfortable all of a sudden. Maybe that was why, for the first time, I actually understood that I was hearing the compressor. And now it didn't have any business intruding, making all that noise. So I went over and turned the damn thing off. I also looked to see the figures in the back. The register read 1313.9. Five more minutes and the double thirteens would have been past.

I went downstairs and phoned Dmitri's house and told them to bring Chris right over. Of course, this time he knew exactly what had happened, and he was crying when he stepped into the house. "Alex just died, Chrish," I said, pronouncing his name like that, just as she always did.

Then he went up to see her. He was crying so hard. He went over, and he kissed his sister, and he told us that she was already getting cold. That was true. But I'll tell you something else. There was more sweet life to her face then than ever there had been in the last long grasp of her disease, the one they never found a cure for.

"Alex was something, Chris," I said. "Your sister was some piece of work for this earth."

"I'll never forget her. I promise. I won't ever." He studied her, there on her bed, where he had always slept with her. "I'd just like to keep her here forever, in a glass box, so I could always see her."

And then Carol and I left the room because Chris asked if he couldn't be alone with Alex for a while.

And that was how my baby girl died, of a long illness, at three-fifteen in the afternoon of Saturday, January 19, 1980. She lived with us almost ninety-nine months, just short of three thousand days. She was dear and noble, and nothing ever controlled her.

CHAPTER 26

We buried Alex three days later, Tuesday morning, January 22. For pallbearers, we chose men who represented various important elements in her life: Wendy's father; the custodian at her school; two of the officers from the Association of Tennis Professionals; uncles from either side of the family; her doctor—people like that.

There were many children present in the church, and it was a lovely short service. Father Shipman praised Alex, he read some of Malcolm Boyd's prayer for her, and we sang "I Sing a Song of the Saints of God" and "Jesus Tender Shepherd, Hear Me," and then, at another point, Joan McFarland rose in the balcony and sang "Morning Has Broken."

It was a gray day, Tuesday. It was not at all like the Saturday Alex had died, when the sky was blue. It had grown colder too, and on the way to the cemetery from the church, some flurries began to scatter in the air. This was the first snow we had seen in weeks. It was the first snow in 1980. During the service at the grave, the flurries turned into real snow—they became big, huge snowflakes. They were so big they looked like lace, and it snowed like that all during the service, while Alex was lowered into the ground.

Clockwise, the pallbearers are Dave Braun, Wendy's father; Paul Penner, her uncle, Carol's brother; Bill Betts, school custodian; Harvey Clapp, one of my best friends; Uncle Gill Deford; Tom Dolan, her doctor; Bob Briner, head of the Association of Tennis Professionals; Arthur Ashe, ATP president (Briner and Ashe made CF the ATP's charity); and Jay Crawford, Tina's husband, Jonah's father. This photo was taken by Jeanne Ashe, Arthur's wife.

About two minutes after Father Kennedy ended the service and I dropped a pink rose on the coffin, it stopped snowing. Just like that. And it didn't snow again for weeks more. It was as if God had been crying for all of us. That's what I think, anyway.

EPILOGUE

After that, we did the best we could. Holidays, as you might expect, are the hardest. Well, holidays and various anniversaries. And every time a school bus goes by. Tina made sure that Alex's classmates got the Valentines she had made for them, and they all wrote us letters about Alex, too. Sometimes Wendy and Aimee would drop over to check on us. Alex's Corner was fixed up at school and The Imaginating Trunk was dedicated down at the Y. We ordered a gravestone. It has a little angel on it, with a lamb and flowers, and a bird up in one corner.

Alex is buried on a gentle hill, looking down toward the church steeple, which dashes up through the trees when their limbs are bare. But there are lots of evergreens on Alex's side of the cemetery, so it is always shaded and cool where she lies, and the snow clings to her grave long after it has faded away all around. Very near, there is a little boy who was killed by a hit-and-run driver a year before Alex died, and just down the slope from her is buried a teenaged girl who died of cancer a few months later. More children die than you would imagine; they do; really they do. The two little girls with cystic fibrosis to whom Alex was closest at the hospital also both died shortly after she did. "It was a bad winter," Tom Dolan told me. "Some of them are real bad." And then, not much later, Tom lost his own youngest son in an accident.

Recovery is uneven. Chris was pretty good the first few months after Alex died—children are resilient and all that—and then one night he was staying at a friend's house, and *The Wizard of Oz* was on television. That was Alex's favorite movie, and Chris couldn't bear things and had to call up and come home. Not long after that, Carol found him silently going through Alex's "jewelry" one afternoon, fingering it, staring at it, sniffling, and after that he went through a rocky few months. Carol and I must never forget (as Alex understood before anyone else) that while we lost one of our children, Chris lost his only sibling.

But he seems to have come out of it pretty well by now. He can't stand to go by the grave, though. He just doesn't like that. I'll tell him I'm going out there, and he'll say, "Well, Daddy, you say hello to Alex for me." On special occasions when we all go to the graveyard as a family, Chris sometimes chooses to stay at the car. On Alex's first birthday after she died, what would have been her ninth birthday, we went down to the beach and set off fireworks in her memory. That made more sense to Chris than standing in front of some dumb gravestone. You just have to do what is best for you. It's good, too, that different things, different times trigger the greatest expressions of grief from Carol or Chris or me. It's best that we're not the most upset together. Then we can help each other out.

It is common, it seems, for many parents to suddenly "see" their dead child, walking down a street, or some other typical place. But that has never happened to me or to Carol. On the other hand, Alex is never far from my mind. We talk a lot about her—"Boy, Alex would have loved that," that sort of thing—and I talk to her sometimes, to calm myself down or to encourage myself. And so much reminds me of her. When I travel, when I am away from familiar things, she fades some, but then when I come back home, she bursts back upon me, and often I start to cry openly when I'm driving the last mile or so home, because, damnit, she should be there to greet me, and she won't be. That's when I feel most sorry for myself.

Some cystic fibrosis parents warned me that the second year could be even tougher. It's hard to tell. I really only know this one thing for sure:

There are no lessons to learn from having your child die. There is no value in it whatsoever.

On May 31, four months after Alex died, Tina had her baby. And it was a girl. Alex had been feeling a baby girl in her belly. She was named Kate Alexandra, as Tina had promised.

Not long after that, Carol came to me one day and asked what I thought about us trying to adopt a baby girl. I said I didn't think much of that at all, but I would consider it. If you want to know the truth, I was humoring her. I thought she was responding emotionally to the arrival of Kate Alexandra, and she would get over it soon enough.

But she didn't. She kept bringing it up. I told her that a baby would foul up her life a whole lot more than mine, especially since here she was finishing college and planning on getting a job, but Carol replied that she understood all that, and still she wanted to adopt. I said, all right, ask Chris. He said it sounded like a neat idea, could we order a brother about two years younger than he was, who was very good at baseball? Well, no, that wasn't exactly what your mother had in mind. Okay, he said, barring that, a baby sister would do fine.

I still wasn't keen. I didn't think I could start all over again as a daddy. But finally I told Carol that a baby had to be completely healthy, with no complications of any sort, and it had to be a newborn infant, and I reminded her that the chances of us getting such a baby in the United States were nil. But at least I had cracked the door; I had said yes, sort of.

Still, I knew in my heart that I was cool to the idea, and as long as I was, it was wrong to pursue it. I tried to figure out why I was so reluctant to consider adoption, and finally one day, when I was out at the grave discussing this with Alex, I understood: I didn't think it would be fair to Alex. She was my daughter, my child. She had been the one born to grow up in our house, in our family. Bad enough that she should be sick and die; now we should haul someone else in, some stranger, to take her place? To me, that would be the ultimate inequity, the final injustice. I just couldn't bring another child in to replace Alex, and, finally, I told Carol that, directly. That was the end of it. I was sorry, but I couldn't do that.

Carol didn't say anything. I went on. Somehow, worst of all, I said, was the way Alex always loved little babies, and she would love a little baby girl the most of all. So here she not only would be replaced by a little girl—that was bad enough—but also she would be the one of us who couldn't enjoy the little girl. That made it crueler still.

Carol just listened to me. It was a lovely summer evening, and we were sitting out on the patio, having a drink. Chris was off somewhere in the neighborhood, playing ball. This is the way it always had been. He would go off, but Alex would get all dressed up in her summer finery, snap on a hundredweight of assorted costume jewelry, and come out and have a Coke with us. Sometimes she would put on her Chinese lounging pajamas and act particularly grown-up. It would be fairly soon after her evening therapy, and she probably wouldn't have to cough unless something made her laugh real hard.

"I'm sorry," I said to Carol. "Do you understand? I just can't do that to Alex."

"You know," Carol said, "if we did get a baby—if—"

"Carol, you heard what I said."

"Just listen to me. If we did get a baby, you know we could never get one in the States, and it would have to come from some country way out of the way."

"I know that," I said. "A lot of them come from South America now."

"Some very poor country," Carol said, and I nodded. Then suddenly, she reached over and took my hands in hers. "Do you remember Alex's prayer, what she said every night?"

"Sure I do."

"You remember the part she made up herself, the part she'd always say: 'And God, please take care of our country, and bring some of the poor people to our country, and make the other countries rich like us.' " There were tears in my eyes even before Carol had finished. A baby would be an answer to Alex's prayer as much as it would be our new child.

At that time my brother Mac, who had been Alex's godfather, lived in Manila, in charge of the Merrill Lynch office there. When he and Zehra and Benjie came back to the States for a long visit that summer, we decided to take advantage of their position and contacts, and before we started going through the South American channels, we asked them if they thought they could get us a baby girl in the Philippines. Both Mac and Zehra said they were sure that would be an easy task, and they would call us as soon as they got back to Manila and got something worked out.

As they discovered, though, while there is immeasurable poverty in the Philippines, and while many orphan children must shift for themselves—and also, while just about everybody over the age of puberty wants to go live in the United States—the Filipino culture is not at all keen on having its native children leave the country. The weeks went by. As we would learn, Mac and Zehra were putting off calling us to tell us definitely that they couldn't possibly get a baby. It was out of the question.

But they had put out a lot of feelers, and one of them reached a prominent Philippine woman named Marietta Santos. Mac and Zehra had never even met Marietta, but she learned of their inquiries, checked them out, and then called them on the phone. Marietta had her own family, but she had herself adopted an orphaned baby boy not long before, and so she was familiar with the local adoption grapevine. Sure enough, about this time, early in September, through a series of tenuous contacts, the wife of one of Marietta's servants heard about a baby that was about to be born out of wedlock to a young girl who was attending school in Manila. She came from one of the other islands, and nobody in her family back home was aware that she had had a brief liaison with a visiting Japanese businessman. And so the word reached Marietta: Did she want to adopt another?

No, she didn't, but she knew someone who did—the wife of a diplomat from a country in Southeast Asia. When the baby was born on September 7, Marietta called up the diplomat's wife. She could have a healthy baby; did the woman want it? What sex is the child? the woman wanted to know. Marietta told her it was a girl. Sorry, said the ambassador's wife, they only wanted a boy.

Marietta had other names on her list, but she decided to call Mac and Zehra next because she recalled Zehra having told her about why we wanted a child—a girl specifically—because we had lost our own. She found their telephone number. It was late Sunday afternoon, and Mac and Zehra were outside barbecuing steaks for some friends when the phone rang. "All right," said Marietta, "I have a beautiful, healthy little girl, and if you want her, you must take her into your house tomorrow."

Zehra gulped and ran to tell Mac of the situation. "My God," he said. "A baby? Tomorrow?"

"That's right," she said.

"Okay," he said, and they went out that night after the barbecue and bought diapers and baby food and all the other things they suddenly needed for a newborn baby thrust into their house. The next morning, barely thirty-six hours after she had been born, our baby girl arrived at my brother's house. She had been taken out of the clinic, driven across town in an open Filipino bus known as a Jeepney, spent the first night with Marietta's servants, and eventually wended her way to Mac and Zehra's. She would be a poor person without a family taken from a struggling country halfway around the world and brought up in America. If she had been a boy, she would have grown up in Southeast Asia. But for chance piled upon coincidence to the point of whimsy, this incredible link of luck and grace could never have been forged.

Mac called up and told Carol that we had a baby girl. We named her Scarlet, because it was pretty, unusual, and distinct, all the things she was, and for her middle name, we chose Faith, which was, of course, for Alex.

Unfortunately, getting title to Scarlet Faith and getting her out of the Philippines were trickier still. God may work in many miraculous ways, but even He seems still to be stymied by bureaucracy, wherever in the world. At first Mac said he'd just fly back with Scarlet early in November when he had to come over to the States on business. Everything would surely be taken care of by then.

But there were some problems. So we decided that Carol would fly over later that month and bring Scarlet back around Thanksgiving. That seemed appropriate.

But as we passed Alex's birthday, sending up the fireworks, and then as November wore on, the red tape multiplied in Manila. Still, Mac remained optimistic and assured us that the Filipino lawyer was moving things along and that

213

Carol could come over and pick up Scarlet and get her back to Connecticut in time for Christmas.

Christmas. Now we couldn't avoid it. The first Christmas without Alex was going to be horrible, anyhow. We had talked sometimes of what we might do to escape all the memories that would flow back with a typical Christmas at home. And so, why not? All three of us would go to Manila to pick the baby up over Christmas.

And that is how we all ended up in Hawaii, where Alex had always wanted to go. We stopped off there to break up the long trip. Carol did not tell me, but she had taken some of the pink sweetheart roses from Alex's grave and pressed them, and then when she found that we were going to Hawaii, she brought them along, and by herself she took them and went out on the beach at Waikiki, and tossed them to the winds, as you would scatter ashes. That is the part of Alex that finally came to Hawaii, the flowers off her grave.

Then we were off on the final leg, to the Philippines. But still there were delays in getting Scarlet out. We had reservations to come back right after New Year's, but even with Marietta's help, steering us down all the right bureaucratic avenues and circumventing some of the more difficult roadblocks, the maze grew all the more confounding. Finally, Chris and I had to leave Carol with Mac and Zehra and Benjie, and the two of us flew back to Westport, to school and work. The days passed, as Chris and I subsisted on pancakes and Burger King, and soon it was January 19. It was three-fifteen in the afternoon, Alex had been dead a whole year, and I didn't feel any better.

Chris and I bought more pink sweetheart roses, and we went out to the grave and laid them there. Some other people had brought her flowers, too, and it was especially pretty in its way, because this was a normal winter and there was snow on the ground to lay the pink flowers on. We stood back and looked at her grave. "You know what I found out, Chris?"

"No, what?"

"I found out that after Alex understood that she really was going to die, that the one thing she worried about most of all was you. She told people that she was afraid about you having to be alone, without any sisters or brothers." He hugged me and shook his head in wonder.

"I never knew that, Daddy."

"Alex loved you so much, kid."

"I think she would have loved Scarlet just as much, though," he said.

"Yeah, well, if she does love Scarlet, I wish she'd discuss things with some Filipino angels and get them to straighten out that mess in Manila." And I put my arm around Chris, and we trudged back to the car through the snow. We sprang for a steak that night, too.

The next day was a Tuesday, Inauguration Day, the day the Iranian hostages were released, but I was beginning to feel that my wife and would-be child were the newest international prisoners. Then, out of the blue, a couple of minutes before Ronald Reagan was sworn in, Carol called from Manila and said that suddenly everything had come together, Marietta had straightened out all the Philippine details and Mac had sifted through all the American triplicates, and she and Scarlet had been cleared for takeoff on Thursday. That was the twenty-second. They would fly across the date line and arrive back in the States on the twenty-second, too.

The plane was on time. Scarlet Faith went to sleep that night in Alex's room for the first time, exactly one year to the day after we put Alex in the earth. There were four of us again, but I think we added up to more than the sum of the parts you could see.

• • •

215

A couple days later, I bundled Scarlet all up and took her out to the grave. There was still snow on the ground, but the roses had pretty much died, so I cleared them up and put one of them in Scarlet's chubby little grasp. And I told her this—and I told Alex for her to listen up, too—that I would never ask Scarlet to be Alex, I would never expect that, but I would tell her all about Alex, and I would expect her to try and live as Alex did, as sure as her mother and her brother and I myself always try to live like Alex, live up to Alex.

And I said, Scarlet, as lucky as we are to have you here, you are also very lucky to be here, and a lot of wonderful people made this possible, especially your Aunt Zehra and your Uncle Mac and Marietta, but their goodness is their reward; they need nothing more than to know that they helped bring you here. No, I said, the only person you really have to feel indebted to is your sister, because she is your guardian angel, looking down on you from the stars. You see, Scarlet, Alex never did get her wish—not the real one—but at least she did get her prayer answered, and that turned out to be you.

Scarlet had probably never been out in the cold this long before, but then she had been riding along in a Jeepney through the streets of Manila before she was a day old, and was no worse for that, and she'd flown halfway around the world, coach, and she was obviously a real rugged, laissez-faire kid, and she took this all in, making sure to keep hold of that rose in her mitten. But it was time to get back inside, and so I turned and started tramping back through the snow, carrying Scarlet and the old flowers. Suddenly I felt I had to stop, though. I looked back at Alex's grave, and I just said, "Isn't this something, Alex? Can you believe this is what really happened?"

And, oh, I can hear her laughing—and laughing real hard, too, but never once having to cough at all: *Oh, my little Daddy . . . my little Daddy!*

"Well," I said then, "okay, we'll just have to start up again and go on from here, but thank you very much, Alex, because we do have a great deal more to work with since you came our way."

This portrait of Alex was taken before the disease began to get at her. I've always thought we could extrapolate from this how she would have looked as an adult had she lived.

AFTERWORD

The most wonderful thing is how many people still remember Alex—even seventeen years after she died. People are still touched by her story and all that she stands for. There is some peace in that. I hope Alex knows what a precious example she has been.

After this book was originally published, a paperback version was issued and then ABC-TV made a movie of Alex's story. In fact, Dave Braun, Wendy's father, who worked for General Foods, was very instrumental in having his company sponsor the film as a Golden Showcase Production.

The film was produced by Leonard Goldberg, one of the most admired men in Hollywood, but, frankly, I was scared to death when I signed over the rights to him. As long as I myself was writing about Alex and my family, I was in control, but for the film I had to cede that authority.

As it turned out, I needn't have worried. Leonard and all the people involved were so sensitive. They also made a terrific movie. A young actress named Gennie James played Alex, with Daniel Corkill as Chris. Bonnie Bedelia was cast as Carol and Craig T. Nelson as me. Yes, it's very weird to watch somebody being you and saying things you said and doing things you did, but we all found the movie to be such a lovely tribute to Alex that we learned to tolerate those bizarre, self-conscious feelings.

The movie was filmed in Toronto in 1985, and the four of us went up for one day to watch the proceedings. Leonard gave Chris an extra's role, for which he made something like a hundred bucks (and is now within two degrees of separation from Kevin Bacon). The movie was so well received that it was shown again on the network. I also know that it has appeared on television in many other countries, because I've had letters from all over the world from people who've seen Alex's story.

This book originally went into four printings in hardcover and another large paperback printing after the movie came out. There has also been a French language edition, *Alexandra: Espoir de Vivre*. (I think Alex would have particularly liked that continental touch.) The book was honored with a Christopher Award, and, altogether, I know that tens of millions of people have either read or seen the tale of Alex's life.

Her death was not just in vain, for she made cystic fibrosis a disease that is so much better known. There are so many terrible tragedies in the world that sometimes they blur before even the most caring of us. Well, Alex gave to cystic fibrosis a face. God bless her.

At the time the book came out, the Cystic Fibrosis Foundation was raising a little more than $15 million a year. Now we raise in excess of $90 million annually, and it is precisely that money that we have been able to use to finance research that has brought us—as I wrote in the foreword—to the cusp of a cure. I don't mean to suggest that Alex was herself responsible for this great leap forward. The two men who have run the Foundation as its presidents—Bob Dresing and Bob Beall—have spearheaded the effort, attracting the many fabulous doctors who have been responsible for the advances in cystic fibrosis research. But Alex was the symbol, and we didn't have that before.

People always want to know why I continue to serve as chairman of the foundation. Well, yes, there certainly have been times when I have grown weary or despairing of struggling with this awful disease—times I wanted to run and hide from any thoughts of cystic fibrosis. When that has happened, though, Carol has always propped me back up. "We're too close to the end," she says. "We can't let Alex down now." Moreover, there are also so many wonderful board members I've served with through the years, and we support each other in this fight.

Our family has managed to endure our great loss. Certainly, though, we were most blessed that Carol convinced me to adopt, because Scarlet has been such a treasure. It helps, I think, that while she is, in many ways, reminiscent of the sister she never knew, Scarlet is also very much her own distinct personality. (This did not, however, stop Shirley MacLaine from blithely telling me once: "Can't you see, Frank? Scarlet is Alex." Oh.)

Anyway, as I write this now, Scarlet is finishing up her junior year at St. George's School in Newport, Rhode Island. She is (if you will forgive a proud father) beautiful, popular, bright, and (most of all, like Alex) so caring of others. Scarlet is also physically strong and agile, incredibly healthy, and a terrific athlete. She has been a top-grade junior equestrian, a varsity swimmer, tennis player, and soccer player, and now she has taken up ice hockey. This, I tell her, surely makes Scarlet the only person of Filipino descent, male or female, who has ever played ice hockey. Scarlet's greatest passion, however, is painting, and she hopes to concentrate on art at college. I believe that Alex would both adore Scarlet and be terribly proud of her.

Chris moved to Colorado after he finished high school—first mostly to ski and then to go to college at Colorado State, from where he has just graduated. He worked extensively for the Denver chapter of the Cystic Fibrosis Foundation at an internship, work necessary to obtain his degree. Chris has grown to my height—six-foot-four—but he outweighs me now, and he hits a golf ball 280 yards, sometimes straight. He has never been able to make himself read this book about Alex, and neither has he ever been able to comprehend how the experience of having your only sibling die has affected his life. "I can't really tell, Dad," he explained to me once, "because that was the only childhood I had."

I *am* pretty sure that it was living with Alex that made Chris more thoughtful of people less fortunate; also, me think the experience made him more wary, less likely to take things for granted. It's also been so gratifying for Carol and me to be able to see the close affection between Chris and Scarlet. (He's simply *Chris* to her—not *Chrish*; that was just Alex.) Since there is an eleven-year difference in their ages, it's perhaps more like an uncle-niece relationship than it is brother-sister, but, whatever, they're the best of friends and hang out like buddies whenever Chris comes back on vacation to Westport to visit the family.

After Alex died, Carol concentrated even more so on her education, first graduating from Sarah Lawrence and then getting her masters in social work at Fordham. She has worked with international students and is now involved in a program where she helps teach inner-city kids in kindergarten and first grade. Carol still looks like Linda Evans; it's just that Linda Evans isn't so famous anymore.

I left *Sports Illustrated* in 1989, but I still work primarily in sports journalism. I do more of my work in radio and TV than I did when Alex was alive, but I write columns for *Newsweek* magazine, and I'm working on another historical novel. My last novel, *Love and Infamy,* took place in Japan before Pearl Harbor, and part of my interest in that subject came, I'm sure, from having an Asian daughter. Your children direct you, I suppose, even as you try to guide them. I also did an article a few years ago for *Conde Nast Traveler* magazine, when Carol and I took Scarlet back to the Philippines and let her enjoy a peek at the culture of her birth.

Chaucer died not long after Alex did, and soon enough after that we found a new home for Buffalo; he was just too hyper a little beast. Chris took up with cats in Colorado and convinced us to try them instead of dogs. We have two now: Tabasco Cat and Jamaica. We live in the same house that we moved into in 1974, the same house where Alex died on that January day that seems, yet, both so near and far.

Occasionally, I run into the children who were Alex's little contemporaries, but who are grown-up now. Jake Weinstock has even become famous for starting a Gold's Gym in Moscow. He's been written up in *The Wall Street Journal* and all sorts of magazines. Wendy Braun got married last year. It happened to be a weekend when Carol and I had to be away, up at Scarlet's school. In a way I was very glad, because I know I would have cried too much at the wedding. I would have been a wreck. You see, the most painful memories are when something forces me to consider how Alex might be today—and how she never got the chance to see today. That is the worst. Last October 30 would have been her twenty-fifth birthday, and I cried off and on all day long.

The Spenglers have moved away from the old neighborhood, and so I hadn't seen Aimee in a couple of years, since she moved into an apartment in New York, but a few days after Alex's birthday, Carol and I got a letter from Aimee. This was the heart of it:

> I don't know why I felt compelled to write to you this October 30, because each one sends me reeling backward, to three little girls, pretending, acting, laughing, and trying out personalities.
>
> I guess I just wanted you to know that Alex and my memories of her mean a great deal to me. She had a profound effect on my life. Childishly, I'd like to think she is still watching me grow up.

So, then Carol and I had a great cry together.

Greens Farms School was closed down several years ago, but they moved Alex's Corner to another school. Along with the Imaginating Trunk, down at the Y, there is also an annual Imaginating Ball in Washington (a CF benefit), and in Columbus, Ohio, some wonderful people opened an Imaginating Studio for the purpose of inspiring young actors. In Des Moines there's an Art for Alex exhibit. Carol and I contributed some beautiful original seasonal banners at our church in Alex's memory.

Many schools around the country assign *Alex: The Life of a Child* as a reading assignment for the whole class. Ironically, that is how Scarlet came to read the book—in sixth grade, I think. Often, then, each of the children will write us a personal letter, which is always a sweet surprise when the packet of letters arrives. Some young people send me term papers they've written about Alex, and on a few occasions I've spoken at a hospital to the young doctors and nurses on the subject of dealing with seriously ill children and their families. In fact, Tom Dolan invited me to speak at Yale–New Haven one time a few years back. I saw Dr. Dolan a few months ago, too. He has retired from the CF clinic, but he still plays golf, bravely, and still cheers for the Red Sox, futilely.

At least once or twice a year Carol and I get a letter from someone informing us that they have chosen to name their child after Alex. It's certainly a more popular name, now. Here, for example, is part of one letter:

> I was born September 23, 1971. When I was sixteen years old, I read a book for the first time, *Alex: The Life of a Child*. I was very touched by the story of Alex's life, but even I could not know to what extent I would come to feel connected to her.

I have never known anyone who had cystic fibrosis. In fact, I had never even heard of the disease until I read your book. But, for some reason, I felt drawn to this brave little girl. I felt as if I might have known her. That we might've even been friends under different circumstances. Maybe it was because our birthdays are barely a month apart and, had she lived, she would be my age. I felt that a huge injustice had been done, that I had lived to be sixteen, and she had already been dead eight years when I was just learning about her incredible life. Whatever the reason, I was profoundly impacted by the words you wrote about your daughter, and she became alive to me.

Enclosed, you will find a picture of *my* Alexandra, who is six years old today. It is no accident that she bears the same name as your Alex. I chose it because it connotes courage and regal bearing to me.

It thrills me that people could take the time to write such gloriously tender letters to us. Hardly a week goes by, even after all these years, when somebody doesn't read the book and then feel moved to write us about Alex. Often these letters simply tell us how much Alex's story has touched them. Mail also comes from people who themselves have CF or have a family member with the disease. In the last few years, though, there has developed a genuine phenomenon. That is: All sorts of young women write how they have chosen to go into medicine or health care because of Alex. They want to save children, as no one could save Alex. For example:

From the moment I began to read your book, I vowed to myself and to Alex, that I

225

would someday help to cure her disease. Now, my once childish wish to save another child's life will soon begin to become a reality, the day I enter college, next fall. I believe I have the capability and tools with which to succeed, and Alex has given me the ultimate determination: to become a doctor.

Or this:

I am currently a student at Washington University, majoring in biology. I have a pre-med concentration, hoping to one day go into genetic research.

When I was seven years old, I saw the movie of your daughter's story. I read the book at age ten. At twelve I volunteered at the CF clinic. . . . I wrote my college entrance essays on your daughter's influence on my life. When people ask me what I want to do, and why, I tell them about Alex. Thank you for sharing her story. It has given my life direction.

Or this:

I always knew that I wanted to work with people, but I wasn't sure how. After reading your book, I thought that I would love to work with sick children, to help them. I thought that I wanted to be a nurse, but then I heard of Child Life Specialists, people who are there in hospitals solely to help children to cope. Just this past semester I did an internship . . . and although it was often sad, their spirit was so beautiful, and, comforting them, so wonderful. All through this I thought of Alex, and I wanted you to know how her legacy continues on.

In fact, it's best now that I let others express themselves through Alex. What more can I say? Here, for example, are some excerpts from the letter of a young woman who wrote Carol and me upon the occasion of Alex's twenty-fifth birthday. She explains that she has had lung problems—not cystic fibrosis—and, as a child of ten, she decided to become a pediatric pulmonologist in order to treat people with CF "because I naively imagined that all people with this disease must be as noble and beautiful as your daughter." She writes how she became a good friend of someone with CF who also had read Alex's book, and:

> . . . We found that we also shared a deep respect for, and emulation of, Alex and her perspectives on life. We have watched the movie together while we've been hospitalized; we have used the book and movie as points of reference for our own experiences (as in "You know, when Alex said . . ."), and most recently, my friend went to Russia and Eastern Europe to examine the possibility of Americans adopting orphaned or abandoned children with CF—and again, we recalled Alex's prayer while making the arrangements.
>
> We have found, interestingly, that a person's knowledge of the details of the movie and the book are frequently a good gauge of his or her humanity. . . . More personally, I just had surgery on one of my lungs, and I was terrified before going into the hospital. But about a week before, I suddenly realized that

227

the day of my surgery was Alex's twenty-fifth birthday. Believe it or not, I was more reassured by this fact than any other as I went into the procedure. My friend with CF has often been to Alex's grave, and she has promised that when I return to the Northeast this spring, she will take me there, as well. It is difficult to place in words what this means to me, but I can only say that it will be a dream fulfilled, to pay my respects and give my thanks to a friend I never met. . . .

Almost everyone I know who has read your book or seen the film has told me that they have at some point asked, "What would Alex do?" or "What would Alex think?" or "What would Alex want me to do?" She continues to live powerfully through the lives of so many people, and I thank you for giving us all the opportunity to know her and to know how much you loved her.

More simply, when I was touring to promote the book, I attended a book-and-author luncheon in Cleveland. After speaking about Alex, I returned to my seat to find a note from Gloria Steinem, who, as the next speaker, had already moved to the podium. It was very simple. It just said: "Dear Frank, Thank you for telling us that even a little eight-year-old girl can be a hero, too."

There it was: Alex is my hero. The only question I really ever have to try my best to answer is: *What would Alex want me to do?*

—Frank Deford,
Alex's father
May 1997
Westport, Connecticut

228